D0810491

JUST

CURIOUS

♦

BOOKS BY
CULLEN MURPHY

◆

Rubbish!
The Archaeology of Garbage
(with William Rathje)

◆

Just Curious

JUST CURIOUS

ESSAYS

CULLEN

MURPHY

A PETER DAVISON BOOK

Houghton Mifflin Company

BOSTON   NEW YORK

1995

For information about permission to reproduce selections from
this book, write to Permissions, Houghton Mifflin Company,
215 Park Avenue South, New York, New York 10003.

Library of Congress Cataloguing-in-Publication Data

Murphy, Cullen.
Just curious : essays / Cullen Murphy.
p. cm.
"A Peter Davison Book"
Includes index.
ISBN 0-395-70099-X
I. Title.
AC8.M895   1995
081 — dc20   94-21671   CIP

All but one of these essays originally appeared in slightly different form in
The Atlantic Monthly. "All the Pope's Men" originally appeared
in *Harper's* (June 1979; vol. 258, no. 1549).

Book design by Anne Chalmers

Printed in the United States of America

BP 10 9 8 7 6 5 4 3 2 1

Printed on recycled paper

FOR
A. M. T.

ACKNOWLEDGMENTS

I am deeply grateful to William Whitworth, the editor of *The Atlantic Monthly,* who commissioned all but one of the essays in this book, and to Lewis H. Lapham, the editor of *Harper's,* who commissioned the earliest and longest. I am also grateful to Corby Kummer, Suzanne Mantell, Deborah McGill, Martha Spaulding, and Barbara Wallraff, who edited the essays; to Elinor Appel, Maureen Brown, Eric Haas, Amy Levine, Amy Meeker, Sue Parilla, Scott Stossel, and Lowell Weiss, who checked the facts; to Peter Davison, who brought the essays together in one volume; and to scores of people mentioned in these pages, who took time out of their day to talk to a stranger.

Contents

◆

CONTENTS · xi

· V ·

MODEST PROPOSALS

—◆◈◆—

Introduction

—◆◇◆—

T H E   S K U L L   A N D

T H E   V O L C A N O

NOT LONG AGO an Italian friend who is a doctor gave me a tour of the anatomical museum at the Ospedale Santo Spirito, in Rome, where he works. The museum is a very old one — Leonardo da Vinci is known to have made drawings there — and the glass-fronted cabinets of polished wood hold specimens wondrous, tragic, and bizarre. As I wandered among the roomfuls of ancient exhibits — skeletons of all sizes and shapes, medical instruments at once terrifying and baroque — I noticed a small display case in an unlit corner. Inside, on red cloth, rested a human skull, and next to the skull lay a small card written in Italian in an elegant antique hand. I called to my friend, who came over and translated. He looked down at the card, and then at the skull, and then at me, and said, "It's Pliny the Elder."

How fitting, I thought. The museum of which Pliny's skull is now a part is just the sort of place that the Roman encyclopedist and author of *Historia naturalis* would have found congenial. Pliny was a soldier, biographer, historian, collector, and student of the natural world in all its aspects — stars and planets, plants and animals, land and sea. His nephew Pliny the Younger recalled that he rarely slept and employed almost every waking moment in writing or study. The quest for enlightenment eventually killed him. Pliny was on a ship off the coast of Naples when Vesuvius erupted, in A.D. 79, and he ordered the ship to shore so that he could see the volcano up close. He did see it up close, and was overcome by fumes.

Looking at the skull, I was struck by an odd thought. It was that the proportion of extant human knowledge ever mastered by one individual may well have reached its apogee inside this very head. Pliny, after all, knew a lot of things at a time when not very much about the world was really known. In contrast, the modern world's stock of things that one might know — data, scholarship, literature, news — is simply too vast to be encompassed, as would be even the trillionth part of it. And that stock of knowledge continues, of course, to expand.

What is one to make of this? An understandable response would be despondency: we are all doomed to inhabit a tiny wormhole of familiar space amid an unimaginably vast and growing unknown. At the same time, the situation offers opportunities: one's chances of bumping into interesting and unfamiliar things by accident have never been better. In recent days, for example, I have learned through utter happenstance that the number of birds killed by domestic cats in the United States in a typical year exceeds the population of China; that modern cooking practices are reducing human tooth size at an estimated rate of one percent every thousand years; that Richard Nixon left instructions for "California, Here I Come" to be the last piece of music played at his funeral ("softly and slowly") were he to die in office; that the earliest document in Latin in a woman's handwriting (it is from the first century A.D.) is an invitation to a birthday party; and that the way to calculate the size of a person's body surface area in square meters is to multiply the person's height (in centimeters) by the person's weight (in kilograms) and then divide by 3,600.

The essays in this book are by and large the result of bumping into unfamiliar things by accident — a piece of news, a random remark, a stray fact, a source of information, a field of expertise — and then pausing long enough to pursue the matter a little further, to see where investigation, or contemplation, may lead. The results are not always serious and not always important, but small subjects can sometimes offer a window onto something bigger. One just hopes it isn't Vesuvius.

I

INQUISITIONS

Going to the Cats

—◆◇◆—

EVERY DECADE or so the United States of America crosses some portentous new threshold that symbolizes the nation's evolution from one kind of society into another. It crossed one after the Second World War, when for the first time in history American men bought more belts than they did suspenders. It crossed another in the mid-1950s, when the number of tractors on American farms for the first time exceeded the number of horses. Now the country faces a new demographic reality: the number of cats in American households has overtaken the number of dogs. According to the Pet Food Institute, a Washington-based trade association, there were about 18 million more dogs than cats in the United States as recently as a decade ago, but today there are 56 million cats and only 52 million dogs. Actually, because millions of unregistered dogs and cats — the illegal aliens of the animal kingdom — go uncounted, it may be that dogs still maintain a slight edge. But sales of dog food are holding steady, whereas sales of cat food have been increasing in recent years at an annual rate of 5 to 8 percent. The trend is clear.

This is not the place to dredge up all the old arguments on the relative merits of cats and dogs, friend of the mouse though I am. But it does seem to me that the displacement of *Canis familiaris* by *Felis catus* might tell us something larger about the condition of the republic, much as from a single drop of rain (to cite Sherlock Holmes's famous example) one might infer the existence of oceans. Consider an America congenial to the dog: it was a place of nuclear or extended families, of someone always home, of children (or pet) looked after during the day by a parent (or owner), of open spaces and family farms, of sticks and leftovers, of expansiveness and looking outward and being outside; it was the America of Willa Cather and Lassie and Leon Leonwood Bean. Consider an America conducive to the cat: it is a place of working men and women with not much time, of crowded cities, of apartment buildings with restrictive clauses, of day care and takeout food, of self-absorption and modest horizons; it is the America of Bret Easton Ellis and *Blade Runner* and the Sharper Image catalogue.

These generalizations may, I suppose, be extreme, but they are prompted in part by a new edition of the *Statistical Abstract of the United States,* which I recently received in the mail. This may be the best book the government publishes, and I wish I could earmark my taxes every year to pay the salary of its editor. According to the *Abstract,* here is some of what has happened to the country from the time when dogs were an overwhelming majority of household pets (I've chosen the early 1970s) to the present day: the amount of land claimed by cities increased by 191,795 square miles, or 49 percent; the number of people living in cities increased by 33 million; the number of households consisting of only one person doubled, to 21 million, and as a proportion of all households increased by 41 percent; the number of families headed by only one parent more than doubled, to 7 million, and as a proportion of all families increased by 100 percent; the proportion of childless couples with both partners in the labor force increased by 9.5 percent; the proportion of working couples with children under three increased by 56 percent; the proportion of new houses having no more than two bedrooms doubled, and the average size of new housing units shrank by nineteen square feet; the number of people living in a typical rental unit declined by 13 percent, to 2.0, and the

number living in the average occupant-owned unit declined by
16 percent, to 2.5; the number of miles Americans traveled an-
nually (including going to work) increased by 631 billion; the
amount of money spent on fast food increased by 153 percent;
membership in the Boy Scouts and the Girl Scouts declined by
25 percent. The *Abstract* carries a lot of other suggestive data.
It provides a recipe, so to speak, for cats.

I do not propose that we attempt to redress the balance. To
be sure, I can imagine certain developments, such as a dramatic
worsening of the many social and physical ills with which dogs
so nobly help us cope, that might foster a resurgence of the
canine population, but this prospect is not, on the whole, very
inviting. By the same token, I can imagine expedient ways of
reducing the feline population to rough parity with the canine
one, although perhaps not without harm to the country's liberal
democratic traditions. In the end, I think, there is no turning
back the clock. As one who has shaken hands with Rin Tin Tin,
I mourn the loss of what was good about dog America. But I
accept the inevitability of cat America, and all that this implies
about lifestyles and public policy. It was hardly a surprise when,
after centuries of dogs in the White House, the most recent First
Pet entered office on little cat feet.

Many Unhappy Returns

---◆◆---

A DECADE AGO the French historian Emmanuel Le Roy Ladurie published a remarkable book called *Montaillou,* in which he brought back to life a peasant village in the Pyrenees as it had existed during the first decades of the fourteenth century. What made the book possible was the existence in the Vatican Library of the Inquisition records of Jacques Fournier, the bishop of Pamiers, who had betaken himself to Montaillou in 1318 to investigate the persistence there of the Albigensian heresy. Fournier, a fastidious man, deposed dozens of people. "In the process of revealing their position on official Catholicism," Ladurie wrote, "the peasants examined by Fournier's Inquisition . . . have given an extraordinarily detailed and vivid picture of their everyday life." The picture is complete down to the kitchen utensils and the hams hanging from the rafters. We learn what people customarily wore to bed in Montaillou, and the etiquette of giving a party, and who employed a wet nurse. All the petty feuds and curious bonds among families and friends are laid bare. With little more than Fournier's records to work from, Ladurie was able to describe a medieval community in just the way that modern social anthropologists now routinely describe living ones.

Jacques Fournier, who became Pope Benedict XII, died in 1342. But his work is carried on, in a way, by the lawyers and judges of an arm of the federal government called the United States Tax

Court. For a fee of $60, any American who has received a "statutory notice of deficiency" from the Internal Revenue Service can go to tax court and mount an appeal. Mostly the cases are settled before trial or quickly resolved in an informal sort of court. But not a few cases, some of which have the potential to set precedents, get a full-blown hearing. Lawyers can be brought in, the petitioner provides an account of his predicament and how he got into it, the IRS counters with its own interpretation, and in the fullness of time a decision is handed down.

The decisions that are citable or precedential are published every month in a series called the *United States Tax Court Reports,* and one morning recently, after a friend alerted me to their existence, I went to the library and settled down with the latest volume it had. By the time the librarians whispered me out into the night, I had read my way back to the early 1970s.

What impressed me most upon looking into the *Tax Court Reports* is the indomitability of the human spirit. To be sure, many of the cases in these volumes involve faceless conglomerates arguing over such things as depletion allowances and investment tax credits, but the cases that really stand out involve private citizens who have decided to stand up for what they believe to be their rights, and who in most cases haven't got a prayer.

I'm thinking of petitioners like Harvey Waldman, a businessman in Marina del Ray, California, who pled guilty to conspiracy to commit grand theft and, in lieu of a one-to-ten-year prison sentence, was ordered to pay restitution to his victims, the cost of which he decided to deduct on his next tax return as a "legal or professional fee." The IRS disallowed the deduction on the grounds that a "fine or similar penalty" was never deductible, and Waldman appealed to tax court, arguing that restitution was something altogether different. Judge Mary Ann Cohen, who heard the case, ruled in effect that the petitioner must be kidding.

Or consider the matter of Arnold H. and Carole L. Feldman, petitioners. The Feldmans lived in Philadelphia, where Arnold was a rabbi. Arnold invited all 725 families in Congregation Shaare Shamayim ("Gates of Heaven") to the bar mitzvah of his son, David, and then deducted as a business expense the cost of the reception. The Feldmans argued that while the bar mitzvah of a lawyer's son might be a purely social event, the bar mitzvah of a rabbi's son "is an integral part of [the rabbi's] professional activities." It was further noted that during the reception certain people had been approached and persuaded to contribute money for thirty new stained glass windows in the synagogue's sanctuary. The tax court would have no part of it. "We do not propose," Judge Herbert L. Chabot wrote, "to set down a general rule in the instant opinion that one can never convert a basic life-cycle family celebration into a business expense. We content ourselves with concluding that petitioners did not succeed in effecting such a conversion in the instant case." Judge Chabot noted that just because John C. Coolidge had sworn in his son as president didn't mean he could have deducted the cost of a subsequent reception.

And here is Biltmore Blackman, petitioner, a resident variously of Maryland, South Carolina, and Massachusetts. Blackman set fire to his wife's clothing (she wasn't in it) after a quarrel one Labor Day weekend, and though he "took pots of water to douse the fire," the fire spread and consumed a house that Blackman owned in Baltimore. Blackman claimed a deduction on his next tax return of $97,853 for a casualty loss that his insurance company, State Farm, had refused to reimburse. The IRS disallowed the deduction and Blackman appealed. The tax court's curt dismissal of the case must have seemed unreasonably harsh to a man who had just been through a divorce. "We refuse," Judge Charles R. Simpson wrote in his opinion, "to encourage couples to settle their disputes with fire."

The tax court judges do have their peeves. They dislike "tax-motivated transactions" that "lack economic substance" — tax shelters, in other words; such phrases as "mining exploration" and "farm losses" and "commodity straddles" are certain to invite scrutiny. The justices are scornful of anyone who claims "reliance on erroneous advice of preparer" as a reason to be excused from tax penalties. They turn deaf ears to those who, in pursuit of constructive engagement with the IRS, have been poorly served by the United States Postal Service. They are understandably impatient with petitioners who have "instituted proceedings for the purpose of delay."

And they are profoundly skeptical of any claims to exemption involving religions that are perhaps not fully in the spiritual mainstream, such as the Universal Life Church, the Church of Ethereal Joy, and the Ecclesiastical Order of the Ism of Am. Lewis Kessler, who lived in Ypsilanti, Michigan, and worshiped the sun god, found this out after the IRS disallowed a deduction of $1,380 for the cost of one of Kessler's "annual journeys to the region located between the Tropic of Cancer and the Tropic of Capricorn (hereinafter sometimes referred to as the tropics) for the purpose of religious worship and prayer." In this case, the pilgrimage had been to Puerto Rico. It is frequently overcast in Ypsilanti, and Kessler argued in tax court that denial of the deduction impeded his free exercise of religion. Judge Chabot, while conceding good-naturedly that "we do not question the sincerity of Lewis' beliefs," ruled against him. "Petitioners are free to practice their religion," Chabot wrote; however, "they will not be subsidized."

I don't know how tax court judges are selected, but by and large they seem to be a sensible, articulate, well-meaning lot. Oh, there are times when the judges wax censorious, and now and again they give someone what clearly seems to be a raw deal. In lots of cases, however, they side with the petitioner. William W. Mattes, Jr., a balding resident of Bel Air, Maryland, was allowed to deduct the cost of surgical hair implants. Donald Givens, a police officer in Los Angeles, was allowed to exclude from his gross income the accumulated sick pay he received following injuries incurred in the line of duty. William H. Horton, of Flint, Michigan, a peripatetic hockey player employed by many different minor- and major-league teams, was allowed to take deductions for related travel expenses and for a subscription to *Hockey News*. Christine Byrne, a clerk in the billing department of a New Jersey company engaged in the sale of steel, was told that she did the right thing in not reporting some of the compensation she received from her employer after a complicated lawsuit stemming from a sex-discrimination investigation. When the issues are not entirely clear-cut, as in the matter of David Cass, an economist at the University of Pennsylvania, the tax court can be truly Solomonic. Justice Julian I. Jacobs ruled on the one hand that Cass, whose specialty was "formulating and analyzing mathematical models of various aspects of economic behavior," was entitled to deduct the cost of the groceries he used while away from home on a fellowship at Caltech; and he ruled on the other hand that Cass's method of determining which proportion of the groceries was consumed by him and which by his wife, two children, and dog — he came up with a formula based on proportionate body weights — was ridiculous. "Any parent having a teenage child," Judge Jacobs wrote, "can attest to the fact that a teenager eats as much as, or more than, the parent regardless of weight." He ordered Cass simply to deduct a sum equal to one fourth of the family's total grocery expenses, discounted by 5 percent "to account for dog food."

The United States Tax Court publishes about a dozen decisions a month. With a full set of these documents, and them alone, historians millennia hence could probably put a big chunk of America back together, with its quirks of mind and taste and law exquisitely rendered. As I left the library, it occurred to me to give a small assist to some unborn Ladurie by making sure that our own inquisition records survive. For all I know, the Vatican Library already gets the *United States Tax Court Reports,* but in case it doesn't, I intend to arrange for it to receive all the volumes for the coming year. Perhaps others will be willing to pick up the tab afterward. There might even be some slight tax advantage in doing so. The work of the Vatican does seem generally to conform to that of a church, and the cost of a donation to this enterprise is surely to be considered a legitimate deduction. I, at any rate, will be declaring it as one, and if the commissioner of internal revenue decides to behave shamefully about the matter, my response will be immediate and unequivocal:

See you in court.

Coming to Grief

—◆◇◆—

THE CALIBRATION

OF MISERY

I OPENED the mail a few days ago to find a letter from a friend, and with it an article from the *Journal of Humanistic Psychology*, which he commended to my attention. The article, titled "Panetics," was written by R. G. H. Siu, who is a chemist, a former director of the Justice Department's National Institute of Law Enforcement and Criminal Justice, and the author of several books, including *Microbial Decomposition of Cellulose*. No sooner had I glanced at the article's abstract than a legal term I had recently heard — "hedonic loss" — came forcefully to mind, along with the realization that hedonic loss might soon have some competition.

I'll come back to panetics in a moment. First, are you familiar with hedonic loss? It is a concept that has by now spread from the federal court system to the state courts, and from lawsuits involving wrongful death to those involving personal injury. Briefly, in wrongful death and personal injury cases the plaintiff used to be able to seek damages from a defendant for loss of earnings, for the cost of medical care, and for pain and suffering, this last category being widely held to encompass such intangibles as "loss of companionship" and "loss of enjoyment." Over the years, however, intangibles have loomed ever larger in the eyes of lawyers and juries, and in a 1984 case that was heard in Illinois, *Sherrod* v. *Berry*, a federal court agreed for the first time that a life's foregone pleasures — the pleasure of residing among one's family, of singing in a choir, of gardening or playing tennis, of a first kiss or a summer day — constituted a whole new category for which damages could be awarded, over and above any award for pain and suffering. In coming to this conclusion the court accepted the argument of Stan V. Smith, an economist from Chicago who testified in the case, that hedonic loss (his term, from the Greek *hedone*, meaning "pleasure") was a legitimate consideration. It also accepted as valid the complex economic models that Smith employed to estimate the monetary value of the hedonic loss involved in *Sherrod*. Smith's economic models needn't be explained here; suffice it to say that they derive from a calculation of the value of a human life, which in turn is based on a cold-blooded, Chicago-school analysis of what Americans, as individuals and through governments, pay to preserve and protect human life. For the purposes of computing hedonic loss, Stan Smith estimated the value of the life of a typical thirty-year-old at between $500,000 and $3.5 million. (His estimates are always presented to juries as a range — what he calls a "zone of fairness.") With sums like these at stake, it is not surprising to find lawyers for the plaintiffs in hedonic loss cases speaking eloquently to juries of life's unfolding pleasures, its vast, ineffable bounty: a Pacific sunset beneath an amber sky . . . a soft breeze caressing a stand of pines . . . the trill of a mountain stream cascading over polished stones . . . the warm unknowingness of a newborn's smile.

I don't have any legal training, and I don't know whether, in terms of justice or efficiency, the concept of hedonic loss makes sense. It has certainly provoked much comment and much opposition. What seems most remarkable about the concept to me, though, is its implicit assumption that the future is to be a friendly time — a period of net pleasure — rather than an indifferent time, a somewhat unfriendly time, or a disaster. It is odd to see lawyers, of all people, making this assumption, given the raw material from which they fashion a livelihood. I remember wondering when I first read about hedonic loss if some legal strategist would soon devise a counter to it, based on the notion that into every life a little rain must fall — might devise, that is, a parallel but antithetical argument, one that might go by the name of pathetic loss (my term, from the Greek *pathos,* meaning "pain"). The aim here would be for a defense attorney to offset an allegation of hedonic loss by showing that a plaintiff, though incontestably the victim of some tragic endeavor or procedure, had as a result of it been spared other kinds of likely and terrible unpleasantness. We have a brush with this very concept every time we say that it's a blessing so-and-so isn't alive to witness such-and-such. There's a hitch, though: would it ever really be possible to assemble data on the average American's level of suffering over a lifetime — data that could match, in some sense, those laid before juries by proponents of hedonic loss?

Enter R. G. H. Siu, whose article is subtitled "The Study of the Infliction of Suffering." Siu's article is a stirring manifesto that, after noting "the unceasing mutual inflictions of suffering by practically everyone," calls for the creation of a new academic discipline, panetics, devoted exclusively to suffering — its causes, nature, and quantification. The name he proposes for this discipline comes from the word in Pali (an Asian language spoken by the Buddha) for the verb "to inflict."

A central feature of Siu's program is the establishment of something called the dukkha (from the Pali word for "suffering") as the basic unit for measuring the level of disagreeability of all things. To get the idea, Siu writes, first apportion all degrees of suffering into a nine-tier intensity scale, ranging from level 1 ("barely noticeable") through level 5 ("interfering with daily life") and on to level 9 ("unbearable, wanting to die"). A dukkha is the amount of suffering experienced in one full day by one person whose suffering is at intensity level 1. Level of intensity multiplied by duration multiplied by the number of individuals involved yields aggregate amounts of suffering. A million dukkhas is called a megadukkha. A billion dukkhas is a gigadukkha. Siu makes no extravagant claims for this conceptual child of his, nor does he sell it short. "The paneticist," he writes, "has good reasons to be dissatisfied with the dukkha as he eyes the rigidly fixed and precisely calibrated calorie of the physicist. But he should gain much comfort as he beholds the wildly varying monetary units of the economist grappling with triple-digit inflation."

Stan Smith, in arriving at his estimates of the value of a human life, used data on spending from a variety of government and private sources. Siu likewise has used data from government and private sources — for example, on unemployment, crime, sickness, poverty, and pollution — to come up with a figure for the total amount of suffering in America in 1979: about fifty gigadukkhas, or 7 percent of the theoretical maximum that could have been inflicted in that year. That is enough to provide every man, woman, and child in the country with suffering at intensity level 5 during the waking hours of about sixty days a year — about right, in my experience.

The relevance to American jurisprudence of Siu's research efforts will of course be obvious, and their utility should become only more apparent as a result of "calibrations and improvements to come." I see no reason, however, why the dukkha must be restricted to the courtroom, the classroom, and the Department of Health and Human Services. There exist many aspects of society whose failings we continue to evaluate by means that seem unnecessarily crude and subjective: movies, plays, and television shows, for instance; books and records; restaurants, politics, fashion, fads, language, technology. Surely the dukkha could serve us well in all these arenas, its range capable of encompassing the painful personal and national impact of everything from the most trifling dental surgery all the way up to voice-mail systems or the return of Linda Ellerbee to network broadcasting. Why mince words? If something's a demigigadukkha, I want to know about it.

The First Brick

—◆◇◆—

SEVERAL MONTHS AGO I came across the work of Ralph G. H. Siu, the progenitor of something called panetics, which is the study of the infliction of suffering. Siu published an article about panetics in the *Journal of Humanistic Psychology* in which he proposed the establishment of a basic unit of suffering, to be called the dukkha. He offered several intriguing calculations based on his conversion of data on unemployment, crime, pollution, and other ills into dukkha equivalents, and he urged the installation of panetics as a new academic discipline at America's colleges and universities — a discipline both theoretical and applied, which would at last give the causes, nature, and quantification of suffering the attention they deserve.

My reaction to Siu's proposal at the time, though I didn't dwell on it in print, can be fairly described as skeptical. Acquiring the means to perform a sophisticated calculus on human suffering could, I suppose, assist in its alleviation. This is certainly the argument that a paneticist would advance. But I worry that suffering may be one of those conditions, like coldness or debt, that an ability to quantify may only make more distressing. Moreover, I am uncomfortable with the idea that in a world calibrated in dukkhas it would be possible to assert equivalences

between certain levels of radically different kinds of suffering —
grief, hunger, illness, and envy, for example — much as in a
world calibrated in dollars one can find paintings, real estate,
horseflesh, and human lives of seemingly equal value. Furthermore, should we not be concerned that panetics could in the
wrong hands be used to intensify rather than alleviate suffering,
and to do so on a scale never before imagined?

Those thoughts, at any rate, came to mind — as did the realization that the whole issue was probably moot. The possibility
that the dukkha had much of a future in academe seemed somehow remote.

Ralph G. H. Siu has, however, been busy. Not long ago I
received a copy of a book by Siu, its spine bound with plastic rings,
titled *Less Suffering for Everybody: A Guide to Panetics*. Along
with the book were some stapled sheaves of paper labeled *Deliberation Distillates,* a newsletter containing excerpts of communications with Siu from forty or so people identified as founding
members of a new organization called the International Society
for Panetics. *Deliberation Distillates,* which serves as an epistolary form of meeting, was inaugurated by a memorandum from
Siu to his colleagues that closed with the charge "And so, my
fellow Founding Members, may the fertile ideas gush forth!"

This package of materials on panetics was sent to me by one
of the founding members, whom I happen to know. He wrote
that the first meeting of the ISP's eleven-member board had just
been held at the Cosmos Club, in Washington, D. C., and that
a plenary session of founding members in Washington would
later officially heave the society into public view. The roster of
the ISP's founding members is a distinguished one, if diverse in
that slightly discordant way for which we reserve the word *mot-
ley*. Although most of the founding members, like the noted
economist Kenneth E. Boulding, have been associated with academe, the group also includes many people from other walks of
life (for example, Patrick V. Murphy, the former police commis-

sioner of New York City, and Gus Tyler, the former assistant president of the International Ladies' Garment Workers' Union). Interest in panetics seems to be nearly as indiscriminate as suffering itself.

I reached Ralph Siu by telephone one afternoon at his home in Washington. He is an irrepressibly affable man of seventy-three who was born in Honolulu to Chinese parents and who retains as legacies of his traditional Chinese upbringing a slight accent and a fondness for proverbs. He spent most of his career in U.S. government service, much of it as the deputy director of research and engineering in the Army Materiel Command. Starting in 1944, he undertook as a hobby what he describes as "the complete psycho-philosophical integration of Eastern and Western ways of thinking." So far six volumes of a projected twelve-volume series on this subject have been published (three by MIT Press, three by John Wiley & Sons). Two others, in what is to be known as the Panetics Trilogy, have been written and distributed informally. One of Siu's earliest books, *The Portable Dragon: A Layman's Guide to the I Ching* (MIT, 1968), was a bestseller and has never been out of print.

Siu speaks with an eager hopefulness that endows even terms like "infliction capacity" and "panetic dominance" with a fetching lilt. He explained that the aims of the ISP, at least at the beginning, are twofold. The first task is to refine the definition of the dukkha and to achieve a consensus on the types of objective and subjective conditions to which it can legitimately be applied. "There's an international unit of vitamin A," Siu told me. "In the same way, we need a standard international unit of suffering we can use for social policy." He stated emphatically that the society was not wedded to the dukkha, which was merely a provisional standard, and added, "I don't want to rule out other options." Assuming, though, that the dukkha, however defined, remains a viable panetic unit, an eventual goal of the society would be to produce an annual estimate of this country's gross national dukkhas as a supplement to other social indicators that are commonly used to gauge trends in the U.S. population's general well-being.

The second objective is the creation of a "panetic systems atlas," which would diagram the various ways in which suffering moves about the world. "Let's take a prison system," Siu said. "On the one hand, you can identify the number of dukkhas being inflicted on inmates in many different ways, and on the other, you can identify all the dukkhas being ameliorated in different ways. So you can map all these streams going in and going out, and make a dukkha-flow diagram. Then you can see where the big dukkhas really are. You might find that where the big dukkhas are is not necessarily what is getting all the attention." The goal, Siu explained, would be to produce such maps for people and institutions of all kinds — for families, workplaces, schools, government bureaucracies, and whole political entities of ever larger size. "Someday," he said brightly, "you could diagram the whole United States. Can you imagine all the thousands, all the millions, of streams of dukkhas going in and out?"

Siu paused for a moment, and then added, "That will, of course, take decades and decades of bricklaying. But someone has to lay the first brick. And it is not just for the sake of knowledge, though there is that. The sooner we put panetics into practice, the sooner some suffering person will be relieved."

Every so often there is a newspaper account of astronomers who have stumbled on some impossibly distant cosmic phenomenon that they believe could represent the birth of a star. In front of reporters, the scientists theorize with barely repressed excitement, intoxicated by the prospect of boundless possibility. That is the tone one encounters in Siu's *Deliberation Distillates*. Needless to say, only time will tell if what we are witnessing is truly the birth of a new scholarly discipline. Many of the telltale signs of such an occurrence are present: the acquisition of tax-exempt status for the society, the intention to apply for grants and otherwise seek "support," the talk of founding a journal, attracting graduate students, holding an international conference. If the idea of the paneticist's dukkha seems to some people too arbitrary or cut-and-dried, so at one time must have seemed the economist's man-hour, the engineer's horsepower. My original reservations were not really put to rest in my conversation with Siu, but I did come away feeling that he was appropriately cast in the role of the Max Weber of panetics — perhaps, indeed, was the only person up to the job.

And what if the endeavor should founder? I expect that Siu will see things in perspective, that he will endure no more than a few dukkhas before equanimity returns. "I don't know if I have a single favorite proverb," he said at one point in our conversation, "but one that my father always told me was 'A full stomach is heaven; the rest is luxury.'"

In the meantime, we can all hope that Ralph G. H. Siu at least brings to a conclusion volume eleven of his twelve-volume series. "It is going to be about cheerfulness," he explained, "which I regard as the pinnacle of harmony with the universe." The basic unit, I respectfully propose, should be called the siu.

New Findings

—◆◇◆—

ONE MORNING recently I opened up a great metropolitan newspaper to the science pages and read an article about a study whose conclusions hit me right between the eyes. "The flippant lines that some men use to impress women," the account of the new research began, "may actually ruin their chances of landing a date." For this study a psychologist at the University of Louisville, in Kentucky, asked local Lotharios to approach unattached women in bars and deploy a clever or flippant conversational opener like "Bet I can outdrink you." He found that a positive response was elicited only about 20 percent of the time. Four out of five women "turned away or asked the men to leave."

Talk about upsetting the conventional wisdom. From the same newspaper on another day: "While gifts can be simple tokens of affection and caring, they can also offer telling clues to the relationship of giver and receiver, social scientists say." And on another day: "Therapists find that when people spend time on themselves they reduce stress, increase their creativity and feel less resentful of the demands others place on them." And yet another: "New studies show that confronting people with the fact that they will die makes them cling tenaciously to their deepest moral values." And another: "Imbalances of power in a relationship can intensify jealousy, therapists say."

There are those who find fault with sociology, psychology, and other social sciences for too often merely discerning the obvious or confirming the commonplace. That the social sciences do this with some frequency is hard to dispute. A recent survey (by me) of recent social science findings, the results of which are being reported here for the first time, turned up virtually no ideas or conclusions that can't be found in Bartlett's or any other encyclopedia of quotations. The findings cited above, for example, had all been widely anticipated, by centuries and sometimes millennia. "When you look at the gift, look also at the giver" — Seneca. "The nurse of full-grown souls is solitude" — James Russell Lowell. "When a man knows he is to be hanged in a fortnight, it concentrates his mind wonderfully" — Samuel Johnson. "Envy always implies conscious inferiority wherever it resides" — Pliny the Elder.

No, originality is not always the strong suit of the social sciences. But is that fact really cause for censure? Or is it, rather, the very glory of the enterprise? Perhaps alone among the disciplines at universities, the social sciences turn up reassuring evidence that life is often just the way it seems. Day after day social scientists go out into the world. Day after day they discover that people's behavior is pretty much what you'd expect. All mature adults possess a mental template of social reality; social science tells most of us that the template is accurate and working fine. This is an enormous comfort.

Most other kinds of research are not comforting at all. Astrophysics, for example, is focused on a domain so inhuman in scale that reports of new findings all lead to one conclusion: our planet is lucky to have been created, lucky to have escaped destruction, and laughably irrelevant. Quantum mechanics? The scale here, too, is incomprehensible, and the message — that our notion of a classic deterministic world is childish — is unnerving but apparently true. Reports from more comprehensible fields are no more reassuring. Earth science? An article in the British journal *New Scientist* indicates that a major and hitherto unsuspected cause of atmospheric warming is the methane produced by cattle, whose numbers have doubled during the past four decades. Medicine? One never has to look far for disturbing news. A letter to *The New England Journal of Medicine* reports the outbreak of a kind of herpes known as *herpes gladiatorum,* which has spread through skin-to-skin contact among college wrestlers wearing a new, abrasive kind of cotton-and-polyester practice shirt. History? A day doesn't go by when illusions are not destroyed about some beloved man or woman, or some event or achievement of which humanity was proud.

So I accept the banality of much social science, embrace its results, and look forward to headlines like "Hard Work Pays Off More Often than Laziness, Researchers Contend," "Love a Key Variable in Marriage, Therapists Believe," "Maverick Theorist Links Immorality, Guilt." Above the level of an atom and below that of a universe, it is heartening to learn, some rules still hold.

Stay the Course

—◆◆—

SECOND THOUGHTS ON

IMMORTALITY

THE FIRST I heard of the Arizona-based self-help group CBJ was during a trip through the Midwest, when I opened up a copy of the *Des Moines Register* and saw the headline "Just Say No to Death." CBJ (the name comes from the first initials of its founders, Charles Paul Brown, BernaDeane, and James Russell Strole) claims that despite evidence to the contrary, it is possible for human beings to achieve physical immortality. To do so, one must have experienced something called "cellular awakening," which is achieved not through lifestyle changes or physical drills but rather through an altered state of mind, one that simply refuses to accept the "death program." "Most people," James Strole was quoted as saying, "actually encourage each other to die, not consciously but unconsciously. We program each other, even from a small child, that you have to die someday, and we prepare ourselves for that because we live in a belief system that death is inevitable." Strole also said, "There is a support system for death, and most people don't realize that."

The existence of a support system for death does seem hard to deny. Looking beyond the obvious — the funeral parlors and cemeteries and crematoria — we see the insurance companies, the doctors, the lawyers. And it gets worse. Examine almost any facet of social organization at all and you come to realize that it is actually *premised* on people's dying at fairly regular intervals. Consider the job market. The real estate industry. The Social Security trust fund. Family structure. Organized religion. Much has been made of the ability of powerful interests in Washington — bankers, dairy farmers, the oil industry — to keep congenial policies inviolate. The death lobby must be the most powerful of all. No wonder immortality has been such a tough nut to crack.

Is physical immortality in fact possible? The article I read in the *Register,* which had been picked up from a Tucson newspaper, quoted two doctors in Arizona who were skeptical of the idea, and I'd probably put myself in the same camp. On the other hand, how do we know that some people haven't been immortal all along, changing jobs, changing languages, changing civilizations, millennium after millennium, even as they maintain a more or less constant appearance? This is the case with the protagonist of Leoš Janáček's opera *The Makropulos Affair,* who, in a life prolonged by an elixir, has had to change her identity with each new generation, from Elina Makropulos to Ellian MacGregor to Eugenia Montez to Emilia Marty. I would not be surprised to learn that Ralph Nader was also such a survivor — indeed, that he was the turn-of-the-century personage we know as John Harvey Kellogg, the inventor of flaked cereal and a promoter of colonic irrigation. I would also not be surprised to learn that Ed McMahon, George Hamilton, and Cher had been alive since the dawn of time, or that Jeane Kirkpatrick was previously the people known to history as Catherine de Médicis, Caligula, and the Maid of Kent. So it may be that immortality has been around for a long while and most of us just never knew it.

If physical immortality were possible, would it also be desirable? This is one of those questions on which snap judgment and mature reflection may never be reconciled. Given the abstract proposition, we would all, I guess, like to live forever, but what happens when one gets down to cases? A considerable portion of the world's literature has in fact been devoted to the subject of immortality, and I spent a few days recently conducting an informal survey. The results were in an odd way reassuring. Although some of the literature, including much recent science fiction, turns out to be in favor of physical immortality, most of it focuses on the darker side of living forever and at least implicitly makes the argument for life — and death — as we know it. Message: stay the course.

From antiquity to the present day, the dark literature has spoken with one voice. Tamper with the rhythms of nature and something inevitably goes wrong. Consider the oft-cited story of Tithonous, in Greek mythology. Eos, the goddess of dawn, asks Zeus to make Tithonous, her lover, immortal. Zeus complies. Eos has forgotten, however, to request perpetual youth for Tithonous in addition to immortality. Tithonous, though immortal, becomes progressively feebler and more senescent. The problem of immortality without perpetual youth shows up again and again. It is the fate, for example, of the struldbrugs in *Gulliver's Travels,* and after an encounter with these hideous creatures Lemuel Gulliver writes, "The reader will easily believe, that from what I had heard and seen, my keen appetite for perpetuity of life was much abated."

Still, there are a lot of characters in literature who have been endowed with immortality and who do manage to keep their youth. Unfortunately, in many cases nobody else does. Spouses and friends grow old and die. Societies change utterly. The immortals, their only constant companion a pervading loneliness, go on and on. This is the pathetic core of legends like those of the Flying Dutchman and the Wandering Jew. In Natalie Babbitt's *Tuck Everlasting,* a fine and haunting novel for children, the Tuck family has inadvertently achieved immortality by drinking the waters of a magic spring. As the years pass, they are burdened emotionally by an unbridgeable remoteness from a world they are in but not of. In one scene Pa Tuck tries to explain to a girl named Winnie, who is not immortal, that living forever is no great blessing. Winnie has just stated stoutly that she does not want to die.

> "No," said Tuck calmly. "Not now. Your time's not now. But dying's part of the wheel, right there next to being born. You can't pick out the pieces you like and leave the rest. Being part of the whole thing, that's the blessing. But it's passing us by, us Tucks. Living's heavy work, but off to one side, the way *we* are, it's useless, too. It don't make sense. If I knowed how to climb back on the wheel, I'd do it in a minute. You can't have living without dying. So you can't call it living, what we got. We just *are*, we just *be*, like rocks beside the road."

To the loneliness one must surely add weariness. In Japanese mythology the character Wa-Sō goes out fishing one day and is suddenly caught in a storm. His boat washes up on a distant shore, the Land of Immortality, whose inhabitants know neither illness nor death. What they do know is a boredom so intense that they pray desperately to the god of death to put an end to their lives — desperately, and in vain. George Bernard Shaw eloquently argued the merits of ever greater longevity in his *Back to Methuselah,* but the playwright himself, age ninety-four, waiting impatiently to die, could be overheard muttering in his garden about "this damned vitality of mine."

The prospect of being overcome by an unbearable weariness runs through much of the immortality literature, and I suspect that few will find the notion implausible. Most of us have had experiences that offer a fleeting hint of what eternity could hold. I have scarcely completed my fourth decade, and yet already certain regular occurrences unfailingly bring on a grim languor, a sense of having been worn down as if by drops of water. I experience such feelings, for example, every time a joyous beer commercial is shown on television. I experience them when exposed to imitations of James Cagney, to the sound of the snooze alarm going off for a second time, to the discovery on the radio of yet another redoubt of classic rock. For some reason I expe-

rience them whenever I hear aging actors on talk shows refer
coyly in anecdotes to "Larry" ("Larry and I were doing *Corio-
lanus* in Shropshire, and — well, he had this scarf, and our little
joke was . . ."). I could no doubt endure another hundred years
or so of all these things. But an eternity?

Coming to the conclusion that physical immortality could be
something we don't really want may, of course, be making a
virtue of necessity. Judging from material I was sent by the group
CBJ, at least fifteen thousand people on five continents have not
come to that conclusion. Those people have taken the pledge —
have just said no to death. A few summers ago many of them
gathered in Arizona for a Convergence to celebrate "an awakening of the body to its true and natural state of being" — that
is, physical immortality. Whether the future they are heading
into is one of happiness and fulfillment or dystopian anomie
remains to be seen. They will certainly have plenty of time for
second thoughts.

As for the leaders of CBJ, I hope they can be prevailed upon
to keep the overall numbers down. Immortality may be a manageable lifestyle option for some small percentage of humanity,
but if embraced by the species as a whole, it would obviously
wreak havoc. Even leaving aside the most obvious drawbacks
— overpopulation, resource depletion, pollution — think of the
potential strain on personal relationships of every kind. Think
of how arduous certain tasks would eventually become — re-
membering names, planning a wedding, breaking into show business. Think of what successive editions of Gail Sheehy's *Passages*
would be like as we surpass age one hundred, two hundred, one
thousand.

You can say what you will about the "death program," but
it sure is good at what it does.

A.K.A.

DOUBLE LIVES AND

THEIR DISCONTENTS

M Y W I F E was absorbed in a crime story in the newspaper one
Sunday morning when she paused to read this sentence aloud:
"They also discovered that he had been leading a double life."
Her head rose from the newspaper. She said, "How?"

I knew what she meant. It was not, How can someone leading
a double life go undiscovered for a long period of time? It was,
How can anyone possibly lead two lives — give comfort to two
spouses, pay two sets of bills, raise two sets of children, rake
two yards full of leaves? It is noteworthy that among fictional
characters who lead double lives, a strikingly large proportion
(Clark Kent, Diana Prince) have been endowed with superpow-
ers — a nod, I now understand, toward realism. Just to make it
through a typical day, almost everyone I know must resort to
the practice known as time-stuffing: eating while dressing, dic-
tating while driving, reading while walking or watching television. During telephone calls the soft click of a computer key-
board being struck now seems to be standard background noise.
There are occasions when, upon being interrupted politely with
the words "Is this a bad time?" I must suppress a giddy, mania-
cal laugh, of the kind Herbert Lom descends into when Inspector Clouseau finally drives him over the edge.

In his book *The Condition of Postmodernity,* the geographer David Harvey argues that Western civilization is in the grip of a phenomenon he calls "time-space compression," characterized by a speedup in the pace of life so unremitting that "the world sometimes seems to collapse inwards upon us." My wife and I recently estimated that far from being capable of leading double lives, we each need about 37 percent less content in the lives we already have. A strong argument can be made for even deeper cuts — scaling back one's affairs to accord with, say, the regime portrayed by John Cheever in one of his journals.

> My weekends went roughly like this. On Saturday mornings, I played touch football until the noon whistle blew, when I drank Martinis for an hour or so with friends. On Saturday afternoons, I played Baroque music on the piano or recorder with an ensemble group. On Saturday nights, my wife and I either entertained or were entertained by friends. Eight o'clock Sunday morning found me at the Communion rail, and the Sunday passed pleasantly, according to the season, in skiing, scrub hockey, swimming, football, or backgammon. This sport was occasionally interrupted by the fact that I drove the old Mack engine for the volunteer fire department and also bred black Labrador retrievers.

Cheever at the time was in his forties, comfortably off but by no means wealthy. He had young children, somewhere. Time-space compression was apparently well shy of its present point of advance. Here was a man with room in his life for another one — which, as we now know, he in fact had.

In real life, of course, people who live double lives almost always turn out to be bounders, and yet there is something horribly compelling about the impulse to which they have succumbed. Stephen Spender, in an essay on the poet Robert Bridges, uses the term "third-person people" to describe those (like Bridges, in Spender's view) whose outward behavior and inner self are exactly congruent — those, as he says, who have no hidden "I" within a public husk of "he" or "she." For most people, though, the alignment between first and third person is never quite exact. Governor Mario Cuomo has on more than one occasion contrasted himself with a fictional WASP counterpart he derisively calls "Mark Conrad." Is it far-fetched to suppose that some small part of Cuomo might actually find Conrad's life appealing? Everyone has at some point wondered idly what it would be like to be someone else. I suspect that most people, too, have given some thought to what name they might adopt if circumstances made it necessary — and have perhaps even fantasized about what such circumstances would be.

In Stephen King's book *The Dark Half,* the protagonist, a novelist who has long written under a pseudonym, tells an interviewer from *People* magazine, "Thinking about writing under a pseudonym was like thinking about being invisible. The more I played with the idea, the more I felt that I would be . . . well . . . reinventing myself." Leading a true double life is an option only for the very few, but the acquisition of a pseudonym offers some of the same rewards at a fraction of the cost. And although the fact has yet to be widely remarked even by anthroponymists, the scholars whose job it is to watch developments in the field of personal names, the United States has during the past few years entered a golden age of pseudonyms. As recently as two decades ago the number of people who regularly made use of a fabricated name, whether for purposes of concealment, aesthetics, or enhanced personal expression, was relatively limited, consisting largely of criminals, authors, nuns, and thespians (but not including Trevor Howard or Fay Wray, surprisingly). Then came the citizens band radio, which in the late 1970s prompted millions of ordinary people to invent "handles" for purposes of communication on the highway. The CB radio prepared the way for an even more pervasive technology — the interactive computer network, many of whose services offer users the opportunity to give themselves pseudonyms. Both technologies have provided the cloak of anonymity, and Americans have shown that under such conditions they hardly need to be cajoled into donning new names — and frequently new personas to go with them. By several degrees of magnitude, more secondary identities are now in play than ever before in the nation's history. They easily number in the millions.

This is uncharted territory, and it remains to be seen what the ramifications will be for the broader social psychology. For one thing, the expansion in the number of people using pseudonyms is occurring at the same time as a subtle but perhaps significant evolution in the way pseudonyms are employed. Formerly, the relationship between real name and pseudonym was like that between the two sides of a coin: if one was visible, the other was not. Increasingly, though, both identities are being deployed at once, as if to suggest that a person's very being has undergone a kind of stock split. A book review in the *New York Times* carries the byline "Adam Smith," and the biographical blurb reads, "Adam Smith, a pseudonym for George J. W. Goodman, is the author of *The Money Game* and *The Roaring '80s*." Formulating the authorship of certain books has become less than straightforward: "By Ruth Rendell writing as Barbara Vine." "By Michael Crichton writing as Jeffery Hudson." "By Anne Rice writing as Anne Rampling."

Is this the future — wielding more than one identity openly and simultaneously? Will parents someday give children a pseudonym at birth ("It was her grandmother's") in addition to the other names they customarily bestow? Tricky issues of etiquette are sure to arise. How will dinner invitations specify which persona's company is actually desired? Should Ruth Rendell be offended if asked to come as Barbara Vine?

Some will look askance at the proliferation of pseudonyms, seeing the potential for existential chaos. They may have a point. Still, the belief that acts of self-creation are not only possible but in some sense what America is all about is one of the oldest strands running through our history. Historians and critics have for more than a century and a half invoked the idea of the

American, pioneer in a vast Edenic frontier, as "the new Adam."
Surely something along these lines animated a recent Libyan
immigrant I heard about on the radio — Bishir Zegman, his
name sounded like — who upon being granted U.S. citizenship
changed his name to Clint Eastwood. It may be appropriate to
see the widespread adoption of pseudonyms in much the same
way — to see it almost as a new form of immigration, one that
in numerical terms happens now to dwarf the influx of corporeal
immigrants. The motives that drive these new immigrants, these
undocumented aliases, are familiar. There is the dream of opportunity, the desire to escape repression. Although pseudony-
mous entities may not enjoy all the benefits of citizenship, in
some states they can legally obtain a driver's license and take
out a marriage license. As has been the case with previous waves
of immigrants, some pseudonyms will end up inhabiting ghet-
toes (mostly in cyberspace) that are not well integrated into
mainstream American life, speaking their own language, main-
taining strange customs.

No doubt some people will end up being swallowed by their
pseudonyms entirely, as people have been in the past, forsaking
that spent husk of "he" or "she" for a newly invented "I."
Recently there came in the mail a new book, *Scram: Relocating
Under a New Identity,* written by a lawyer named James S.
Martin, which offers practical tips on how to slip the tightening
bonds of present circumstance in an irreversible and undiscover-
able way. This is not, of course, something I would actually do.
But I must confess that now and then when I hear the words "Is
this a bad time?" my eyes stray unbidden to *Scram.* A bad time?
No, it's not a bad time. In fact, it's now or never.

The People's Business

—◆◇◆—

E VERY YEAR at about the middle of April I find myself making a trip down to the John Fitzgerald Kennedy Federal Building in Boston to obtain the form for an automatic extension of the deadline for filing an income tax return — a form that the administrators of the Internal Revenue Service don't see fit to include (and I can hardly blame them) in the standard packet that arrives at residences every January. I am always surprised at how much I end up enjoying this trip, despite the inconvenience it involves and the financial hemorrhage it sometimes portends.

The truth is, there is a certain grandeur in these federal buildings, which have by now arisen in the downtowns of every large and medium-size and subcompact city in the land. The grandeur is almost never architectural. It derives from the fact that here, in one building, are offices and officials representing virtually every distinct function of the government of the United States — a homuncular version of the entire federal bureaucracy. I once took the elevator to the top of the Kennedy Building and then made my way down floor by floor, walking the hallways just to read the signs. FEDERAL BUREAU OF INVESTI-GATION. ARMY LIAISON OFFICE. GOVERNMENT PRINTING OFFICE. BLINDED VETERANS ASSOCIA-

TION. GENERAL SERVICES ADMINISTRATION. PUB-
LIC HEALTH SERVICE. OFFICE FOR CIVIL RIGHTS.
On any given day families of various hues and from various
points of origin can be seen fidgeting as they wait in line outside
the Immigration and Naturalization Service. In other corridors
military officers stride crisply by. Agency seals enliven walls and
doors.

The Public Buildings Act of 1959 supplied the legislative un-
derpinning for the federal office buildings we have today. Lyndon
Johnson's push for urban renewal and the federal government's
growing domestic activism in other areas provided further impetus. Offices that had once been scattered throughout a city
were now consolidated in a large complex whose erection was
frequently intended to anchor the redevelopment of a decaying
downtown. There were about sixty of these new federal office
buildings in 1965. There are now several hundred.

However maddening the federal government may sometimes
be, the ubiquity of its buildings brings a certain reassurance.
When I arrive these days in an unfamiliar city and happen upon
one of these outposts, I experience, momentarily, the odd sense
of being . . . well, a Roman citizen during the second century
A.D., shortly after Hadrian's building spree. As different as one
city may have been from another, the public core of major population centers bore the unmistakable imprint of Roman rule: the
temples of Jupiter, Juno, and Minerva, the imposing basilica, the
public latrines. One would have felt somehow grounded whether
wandering about in Trier or Cyrene or Leptis Magna — would
have felt, as Gibbon noted, that imperial authority was being
exercised "with the same facility on the banks of the Thames,
or of the Nile, as on those of the Tiber." Wander about inside
the federal office building in Raleigh or St. Louis or Phoenix and
a similar sensation may catch up with you.

If the world inside the federal office building seems to represent the government in microcosm, an obscure publication that
one can order at any government bookstore (the major federal

office buildings usually have one) shows the government in a very different way: with the magnification turned up a few thousand percent. The publication, to which I have grown mildly addicted, is called *Commerce Business Daily*, and it owes its existence to the fact that whenever the federal government needs to procure goods or services valued at $25,000 or more — which it does continually — it must publicly solicit bids. *Commerce Business Daily* is the public record of all this activity (and also of many smaller transactions). In tiny type on cheap newsprint, it announces bids that are being accepted and contracts that have been awarded — bids and contracts for the lease of helicopters by the Interior Department in Anchorage and of washers and dryers by the Air Force in Plattsburgh; for the purchase of graph paper by the National Institutes of Health, of new bassoons by the Air Force Band, of steel-toed shoes for the Job Corps; for tree clearing and snow removal and garbage collection; for software maintenance and offset printing; for demolition; for everything. A friend of mine once came across a solicitation for "red tape." A typical entry reads like this:

Bureau of Prisons, Federal Correctional Institution, Marianna, FL 32446
Installation of Razor Wire. . . . Provide labor and equipment necessary to attach 610 rolls of non-reinforced and 30 rolls of reinforced wire to the fences and grounds along the perimeter. . . .

As one might expect, many of the U.S. government's needs involve the military. "Potato Chips and Corn Chips": a dozen lines give precise specifications for the 132,000 packages of the former and 55,000 of the latter needed by Fort Campbell, Kentucky. "Shell Eggs": the Defense Personnel Support Center, in Philadelphia, is looking to buy 394,360 dozen of them. "Various Football Equipment": a supplier is sought by West Point. "Set, Reset and Realign Headstones at Arlington National Cemetery." "Drydock & Repair, USCGC Wyaconda." "Loose Mine Restraint System." "Insignia, Embroidered." "TV Surveillance and Monitoring System." "Guided Missiles."

Reading *Commerce Business Daily* even for a few weeks (each issue contains five hundred to a thousand notices) gives one an appreciation of how vast and all-permeating an enterprise the federal government is — helps one see it from the point of view, one might say, of someone appointed to be the janitor of the whole thing. And small signs here and there give hints of wider national problems. The Bureau of Land Management one day makes known its need for people to conduct a population survey of the desert tortoise, a threatened species. The U.S. Customs Service puts out the word that it is looking for a company to provide "Laboratory Urinalysis Drug Testing Services." The U.S. Justice Department asks to hear from organizations with experience in computer games technology, because "the department wishes to use role-playing/simulation gaming techniques" to train employees in the "rules and regulations on ethics in the federal government." From time to time there is also cause for modest celebration — for example, the recent cancellation of an order for this item: "Pouch, Human Remains."

Mostly, however, *Commerce Business Daily* pulls one in not by means of what is exceptional but through the sheer scope and volume of what is normal — the mundane immensity of the people's business.

Not long after I became a reader of *Commerce Business Daily,* I began to entertain the possibility of a sister publication, similar in format but devoted exclusively to the management and provisioning of my own household. I am still of two minds about this.

On the one hand, *Murphy Household Daily* could lend a sense of grandeur ("Drydock & Repair, Ford Taurus Wagon") to activities that otherwise might be deemed little more than chores. The publication would also act to reduce impulse buying. The occasional planting of items like "TV Surveillance and Monitoring System" and "Installation of Razor Wire" would also be an ideal way to send subtle social cues to the younger members of the family. So there would be clear advantages.

On the other hand, a record of every item bought and every service used by a typical family during the course of a year could turn out to be, on balance, an oppressive document, its validation of unimaginably vast and varied accomplishments undermined by the knowledge that, most probably, exactly the same things will have to be done again and again for years and years. Knowing what you're getting into has its uses in government. Not knowing what you're getting into has its uses in life.

Order in the Court

—◆◆◆—

J U S T I C E   B Y

T H E   N U M B E R S

A FEW MONTHS ago a friend was elevated from the base munificence of her private law practice to the noble penury of the Connecticut bench. My wife greeted the news with the announcement that she, too, would like to be a judge. I pointed out a few of the usual prerequisites: "One, law school. Two, practicing law for a while. Three, getting involved with politics." She said, "No, no. I want to go straight to the judge part."

Most of us, I imagine, have from time to time entertained similar aspirations. Who has not read reports of a judge letting off a chronic malefactor with a mere slap on the wrist and suspected that any citizen hauled at random off the streets would have devised a more appropriate retribution? By the same token, on those occasions when the headlines report the meting out of a punishment that truly fits the crime — "Slumlord Sentenced to Life in Tenement," say — who does not sense that the forces of the universe have at least for an instant come into harmonious alignment? Who doubts that were he or she to ascend to the bench, such occasions would become less and less rare? Certainly my wife feels that no-nonsense sentencing would be a hallmark of her judicial career, and when I hear imprecations like "Throw away the key!" and "Fry 'em!" tumble from her lips as she reads the morning paper, I am assured that she has not broken training.

The search for a better way to dispense justice lies, of course, at the very heart of the great human drama. And, to be fair, that the record so far is decidedly mixed owes as much to the existence of law itself as to the idiosyncrasies of magistrates. The decision by many societies — a hasty one, some might argue — to abandon the simple blood feud as the basis of conflict resolution led eventually to the embrace of an alternative system, in which a common body of law and custom, jerrybuilt through centuries of venal accretion and bitter compromise, was meant to cover every conceivable situation. This was a recipe, we now know, for perverse incentives and maddening inconsistency.

The problems became apparent very early. Consider the *Pactus legis salicae*, the influential legal code promulgated by Clovis, the Frankish king, in the sixth century A.D. The Salic Law is in the main a hard-nosed and unsentimental document, and a refreshingly unhypocritical one in certain particulars. With its concept of *wergeld*, or "man-money," it was unabashed about asserting that the lives of different kinds of people (young men, pregnant women, slaves) had different monetary values, as compared with the daintier modern practice of letting juries implicitly make similar distinctions while pretending that they don't. The Salic Law also shone the cleansing light of justice into crannies that many of us might have overlooked; for example, "If anyone without the permission of the judge or of him who put it there, presumes to take the head of a man which his enemy had put on a stick, he shall be liable to pay 600 denarii."

Yet even this methodical and frequently admirable document contains much that is unjust or inexplicable and must have given people at the time considerable cause for complaint. Here is one provision: "If anyone strikes a man on the head so that the brain shows and the three bones over the brain protrude, he shall be liable to pay 1,800 denarii."

That sounds fair enough. But wait: if you shoot a poisoned

arrow at someone *and miss*, the fine is even higher — 2,500 denarii, the same fine levied on a person who "cuts another man's hand and the hand hangs crippled." A similar skewing is evident with respect to libel. "If anyone charges another with throwing down his shield while in the army or with fleeing because of fear," the fine, according to the Salic Law, is to be 120 denarii. So why, "if anyone calls another a rabbit," should the fine be twice that amount? Why should the fine for knocking out a tooth be the same as for cutting off an ear or a finger? And it is hard to see how the penalty for personal assault — 120 denarii for each landed punch, but levied only on the first three — could have done anything to limit the severity of such incidents.

I would hasten to point out that such imbalances are by no means confined to ancient history. Living in twentieth-century Massachusetts, I fully empathize with the sixth-century Franks. My state's legal code differs noticeably from the Salic Law in significant details, but in some elements of character differs not at all. I was surprised to learn, for example, that in Massachusetts the maximum fine for throwing litter from a moving vehicle is a stiff $3,000 (first offense). To put that sum into perspective, consider that sending one of my children out on the streets to beg for a day would risk, at maximum, only a $200 fine. Indeed, for less than the cost of tossing a candy wrapper out the window, I could drive all three children to downtown Boston to beg for two days on a holiday weekend ($1,200), sell cigarettes to each member of a second-grade baseball team ($900), steal a box of tools from a construction site ($100), and, while driving twenty-five miles above the speed limit ($200), run over ten cats and fail to report the fact ($500).

This is not to say that no progress has been made during the past fifteen hundred years — that the sharp quillets of the law have become only more inexplicable. Clovis would, I think, have been impressed by the *Federal Sentencing Guidelines Manual,* a three-pound, eight-hundred-page document that came in the mail not long ago. I had ordered this document, which is compiled by the United States Sentencing Commission, after learning about it from our friend the Connecticut judge. The manual represents an ambitious attempt to make the calculation of a criminal's debt to society what it has never before truly been: rational and scientific, coolly consistent, mathematically aloof. In addition to the federal government, perhaps a dozen states have established sentencing standards of one kind or another.

The federal guidelines are, however, without peer. All federal crimes are now listed according to a degree of seriousness, or "offense level," from a minimum of 1 to a maximum of 43. These numbers run down the left-hand side of a page headed "Sentencing Table." From left to right run the Roman numerals I to VI. These represent the "criminal history category," which refers to the degree of incorrigibility of the accused. The sentencing table works somewhat like a mileage chart in a road atlas. To determine the punishment for a particular person convicted of a particular crime, simply move a finger across from the offense level and then down from the criminal history category.

Actually, it's not quite that simple: the offense level and the criminal history category are both subject to dozens of incremental modifications. Was the perpetrator a ringleader or an accomplice? Was he on parole at the time of the crime? Did he abuse a position of public trust? Did he try to obstruct justice? Did the crime involve the abuse of specialized professional skills, such as those of accountancy or the bar? If there was a victim, was the perpetrator courteous and considerate toward this person, or was his behavior pretty much inexcusable? Was the victim elderly or infirm? Mentally impaired? A police officer? Is the perpetrator truly sorry for what he did? Depending on the answers, the judge can add or subtract points. The figuring is done on printed worksheets, which lead one along relentlessly from line to line, from page to page, much the way a tax return does.

Here is how Worksheet D begins:

Docket Number _____

1. Adjusted Offense Level
   (From Worksheet A or B)
   If Worksheet B is required, enter the result from
   Worksheet B, Line 9. Otherwise, enter the result
   from Worksheet A, Line 5.

2. Acceptance of Responsibility
   (See Chapter Three, Part E)
   If applicable, enter "2."
   If not applicable, enter "0."

3. Offense Level Total
   (Line 1 less Line 2)

4. Criminal History Category
   (From Worksheet C)
   Enter the result from Worksheet C, Line 8.

This work culminates in the computation of what might be thought of as Adjusted Gross Behavior. The sentencing table then reveals What You Owe, expressed as a range of months in prison. A person in criminal history category I (basically, someone with no more than one prior conviction, and that for a minor offense) who hijacks an airplane without loss of life (offense level 38) would be liable for 235 to 293 months in prison. The range of possible sentences in the table extends from a low of "0–6" to a high of "life."

No provision seems to have been made for handing down a sentence that in exceptional circumstances my wife has been known to favor: "Nuke 'em till they glow." But as the manual frankly notes, "some offenses that occur infrequently are not considered in the guidelines."

There is, I must admit, a certain technocratic efficiency in the idea of the *Federal Sentencing Guidelines Manual*. In theory, large numbers of miscreants can be processed even as we avoid wide disparities in the calibration of justice. Perhaps one day soon we will also be able to achieve substantial economies by having criminals do the paperwork and file their own sentencing returns, just as taxpayers do. Career criminals might even be made to file quarterly estimates. Certainly the development of a criminal class capable of dealing with forms of this kind — capable even of cheating on them imaginatively — would put paid to talk of American educational decline.

Still, the advent of guidelines cannot help muting enthusiasm for going "straight to the judge part," at least in one whose tastes in justice may run to the poetic. And one can only wonder about what effect guidelines may ultimately have on the very idea of exercising judgment.

I cannot erase a discomfiting image from my mind. It involves Solomon, that wise judge, who in a famous episode had to choose between two women, each claiming to be the mother of a certain infant. He called for his sword. And he . . . well, the passage in the Book of Kings, as I see it now, reads like this: "And the king said, 'Bring me Worksheet D.' And Worksheet D was brought to him."

The Fortieth Parallel

I N   S E A R C H   O F

N O W H E R E S V I L L E

IN THE SMALL TOWN where I live — Medfield, Massachusetts (population: 10,500) — some local actors recently put on a production of *The Music Dreaming Man,* by Bonnie Graves Wilder, a musical that celebrates the life of one of Medfield's most famous citizens, Lowell Mason. Mason was born in 1792 and is known today throughout the town, and perhaps to you, as "the father of music education in the public schools." We're pretty proud of Lowell Mason, as we are of several other prominent Medfield residents, including the historian Hannah Adams (1755–1831) and the painter George Inness (1825–1894).

Medfield was founded in 1649 and has therefore had almost three and a half centuries to produce some famous people. But few towns in the United States have not been in existence for at least a century, a fact that made me wonder, Is there anyplace in America that cannot by now associate itself with a single person who arouses a glimmer of recognition? Is there anyplace that has added not one ingredient to the roiling stew of national celebrity? Is it possible, as the twentieth century draws to a close, that some village or burg might justifiably lay claim to the title Nowheresville?

It would, of course, be difficult to check out every little settlement in the United States; that is a life's work. However, looking at a map one day, I noticed that the fortieth parallel neatly bisects the country from coast to coast and realized that it could provide me with what a trench dug across a large site provides an archaeologist: a glimpse of the big picture. I asked a disinterested bystander to find an atlas and pick out fifty or so towns that lie on or close to the fortieth parallel, stipulating that the towns have populations of 20,000 or less — these being the most likely to inhabit the penumbra of history's gaze — and that they be strung out fairly evenly across the country. A list was duly compiled. Then, starting in the East and moving methodically westward, undeterred by swollen streams and snowbound mountain passes, I began calling up the library or historical society or museum in each town and asking people there if they could think of anyone in the area whose name or accomplishments might have caught the nation's eye.

—◆◈◆—

The fortieth parallel comes ashore, after its nonstop trip from Portugal, a few miles south of the boardwalk at Point Pleasant Beach, New Jersey (population: 5,600). Barbara Kelly, of the Point Pleasant Library, took my call. "Eugene O'Neill married a woman from Point Pleasant and lived here for a while," she said. "His daughter Oona, who married Charlie Chaplin, considered this her hometown. She went to high school here, and everyone remembers her as being very nice." The next designated stop was Burlington (10,300), the birthplace, I learned, of James Fenimore Cooper and Captain James Lawrence (the last words of whose naval career were "Don't give up the ship").

Further inland: Mount Holly, New Jersey (10,800). "Offhand," said Kathryn Heuer, of the Burlington County Historical Society, "I'd have to say John Wollman, the abolitionist Quaker minister." She went off and found a book. "His dates are 1720 to 1772. The financier Stephen Girard had a house in Mount Holly. He's 1750 to 1831. And Peter Hill, the black clockmaker, lived in Mount Holly in the early 1800s." Because my next stop, Palmyra (7,300), was also in Burlington County, I asked Heuer about that town. She said "Hmmm" and called out to someone across the room. After she got a reply, she said into the phone, "Christian Jensen, inventor of the Scoop Washing Machine."

The fortieth parallel crosses the Delaware River at Philadelphia. I picked it up thirty miles to the west, in Downingtown (8,300). Any prominent sons or daughters of Downingtown? "Zebulon Thomas, who was a principal agent of the Underground Railroad," said Flora Jeanne Hoch, of the Downingtown Library Company. "In fact, the Underground Railroad went right through this building. There's an escape tunnel in the basement. Also, Steve McQueen was on location here for a while, because part of his movie *The Blob* was filmed in Downingtown. The diner scene." The next town on my list, Coatesville (11,000), is just down the road from Downingtown, on Route 30. A clerk at the Coatesville Area Public Library didn't hesitate before answering, "This is the birthplace of Susan Richardson, the young woman who was on *Eight Is Enough*." I didn't press; Susan Richardson was clearly just the top of the list.

On to Millersville (7,400), a few miles from the banks of the Susquehanna River. Robert Coley, an archivist at Millersville University's Ganser Library, produced the names of no small number of Millersville's most accomplished natives, among them E. O. Lyte, who wrote the song "Row, Row, Row Your Boat." My final stops in Pennsylvania were Mount Joy (6,000) and Connellsville (10,300). Nancy Dyer is on the staff of the Lancaster County Library. "Simon Cameron, Lincoln's secretary of war, lived just outside of Mount Joy," she said. "Susanna Wright, a

Colonial intellectual and friend of Ben Franklin, lived near Mount Joy. Bruce Sutter, a former pitcher for the Cardinals and Braves, is from here. And Reginald De Koven, who wrote the song 'Oh Promise Me,' lived in the area. It's often played at weddings." I turned my attention to Connellsville, which is about thirty-five miles south of Pittsburgh, on the Youghiogheny River. A librarian at the town's Carnegie Free Library said, "We have Bubba Braxton. He was a football player. And there's a runner who came from here, John Woodruff. There's a park named after him."

Braxton, I knew, was a fullback and a running back for the Buffalo Bills in the 1970s. I didn't know about Woodruff, so I asked my father, who is generally abreast of this sort of thing. "Woodruff represented the United States in the eight hundred meters at the 1936 Olympics, in Berlin," he said. "In the middle of the race, feeling crowded by the pack, he stopped, let everyone run by him, and then passed them all on the outside to win the gold medal. He had the longest stride I've ever seen — maybe twelve feet. He also served under your uncle Bob in the 369th Infantry of the New York National Guard. Nice guy."

—◆◆—

The West Virginia panhandle is only a few miles wide where the fortieth parallel crosses it. I skipped over the panhandle to Bellaire, Ohio (7,700), which lies on the Ohio River just above Lock & Dam No. 13. John Kniesner, of the Bellaire Public Library, said, "Jacob Heatherington settled in Bellaire. He was an investor in coal mines, and the legend 'The House that Jack Built' is based on an incident that involved him." Jean Gwinn, the librarian of nearby Martin's Ferry (9,300), the next town on my list, said, "Our most famous citizen was William Dean Howells. James Wright, the poet, is also from Martin's Ferry. And Lou Groza, a kicker for the Cleveland Browns." Moving across the state, I checked out Cambridge (12,500), Bexley (13,400), and Greenville (13,000). The first of these towns is the boyhood home of the actor William (Bill) Boyd, who played Hopalong Cassidy. It's also the birthplace of the astronaut and senator John Glenn. Bexley, the next town, is where Leslie Wexner, the founder of the retail chain The Limited, makes his home. Lori Greer answered the phone at the public library in Greenville, the last town in Ohio that I called. She said, "The only people I can think of from around here are Lowell Thomas and Annie Oakley. But hey, that's not too bad."

If you go north out of Greenville on Route 118, you eventually cross the Stillwater River and enter Ansonia; if you make a left there, onto Route 47, in a few minutes you'll reach Indiana. The third town you hit in Indiana is Winchester (5,800). Rick and Randy Zehringer — "they later changed the name to Derringer," said Jenny Stonerock, of the Winchester Community Library — and Randy Hobbs came from there; they sang under the name the McCoys and had the hit single "Hang On, Sloopy" in 1965. Another Winchester native is Robert Wise, who produced and directed *West Side Story* and *The Sound of Music*. Moving west: Greenfield, Indiana (12,900). "Well," said Tina Smith, of the Greenfield Public Library, "there's James Whitcomb Riley. He was born and lived in Greenfield. And the basketball player Michael Jordan is from Greenfield." She paused for a second. "No, I'm just kidding about Michael Jordan."

Elwood, Indiana (10,000), a little farther along, yielded Wendell Willkie; the librarian there played the name like a trump ace and made no attempt to say more. I headed for Noblesville (16,900), the birthplace, I discovered, of the mystery writer Rex Stout, and then for Lebanon (12,500). Rosemary Peterman, the town's unofficial historian, had just come in the door. "This was Eugene Pulliam's hometown," she said. "He had the newspaper here, the *Lebanon Reporter*. He was Dan Quayle's grandfather, of course. And Dan Quayle lived here when he was small." Following the fortieth parallel the rest of the way through Indiana took me to Frankfort (15,300), the birthplace of the actor

Will Geer, who played Grandpa Zeb on *The Waltons,* and finally
to Crawfordsville (13,500), the home of General Lew Wallace,
who wrote *Ben Hur.* "Ezra Pound also lived here, while teaching
at Wabash," said Deatra Smith, of the Crawfordsville District
Public Library, who would say no more on the record. However,
she did send me an article about Pound in which he described
his time in Crawfordsville as living "in the sixth circle of deso-
lation."

Only two towns on my list were in Illinois. The first was
Lincoln (16,300). The theologian Reinhold Niebuhr lived there
for a while in the early 1900s, I was told. Also, Langston Hughes
lived in Lincoln as a boy and wrote the class poem for his
eighth-grade graduation ceremony. The second Illinois town was
Beardstown (6,300). The phone at the Beardstown Public Library was answered by a woman who determinedly gave her
name as *Mrs.* Alice Lou Schnake. "Red Norvo is a famous Beardstown resident," she said. "He was a xylophonist and he played
with Benny Goodman's band. That was before your time, I suspect. Still living, though, Norvo is. Must be in his nineties."

—◆◆—

The fortieth parallel meets the Mississippi at the Mark Twain
National Wildlife Refuge and then for a thousand miles lies
more or less flat as it crosses the Great Plains. It transects northern Missouri, forms the border between Kansas and Nebraska,
and then penetrates Colorado, where at Boulder it climbs into
the Rockies. Thirteen towns on my list lay between the Mississippi and the mountains. I went through them with dispatch.

Moberly, Missouri (13,400): home of General Omar N. Bradley.

Brookfield, Missouri (5,600): home of General John J. Pershing.

Chillicothe, Missouri (10,000): home of Grim Natwick, the
creator of the cartoon character Betty Boop; home of Randy
Nosek, a pitcher for the Detroit Tigers.

Trenton, Missouri (6,800): home of General Enoch Crowder,

"the father of the Selective Service System"; home of Burleigh Grimes, a spitball ace for the Pittsburgh Pirates and a Hall of Fame member.

Falls City, Nebraska (5,400): birthplace of the runner Gil Dodds, "the flying parson," a divinity school student and America's top miler in the mid-1940s. ("Not the first flying parson, of course," my father said when I asked if he remembered Dodds.)

Nebraska City, Nebraska (7,100): home of Julius Sterling Morton, "the father of Arbor Day"; home of the business partners Russell, Majors, and Waddell, who created the Pony Express; frequent R&R destination of Frank and Jesse James.

Beatrice, Nebraska (13,000): home of the actor Robert Taylor and the comedian Harold Lloyd; birthplace of the beat poet Weldon Kees, who may or may not have jumped off the Golden Gate Bridge.

Washington, Kansas (14,000): final home and resting place of Charles Becker, who played the mayor of Munchkinland in *The Wizard of Oz*.

Fairbury, Nebraska (4,900): the place where James Butler ("Wild Bill") Hickok earned his reputation as a gunfighter, by killing three men in a shootout.

Fort Morgan, Colorado (8,600): boyhood home of Glenn Miller; final resting place of the science fiction writer Philip K. Dick, whose tomb has become a cult shrine.

Brighton, Colorado (14,700): home of Baxter Black, the "cowboy poet" and *Tonight Show* oddity.

Golden, Colorado (15,500): home of Adolph Coors, the brewer. William ("Buffalo Bill") Cody is buried nearby.

In Yuma, Colorado (2,900), I spoke with Stephen Chaplin, the vice president of the twelve-member Yuma Museum, whom I reached at his place of business, Chaplin Electric. "We have a professional golfer named Steve Jones," Chaplin said. "Last year he won the Bob Hope Desert Classic and the Tournament of Champions." Chaplin thought for a minute and then said, "Did you try Otis, Colorado? They must be near the fortieth parallel. They've got Bob Layher, one of the original Flying Tigers. Did you try Red Cloud, Nebraska? They've got Willa Cather." Apparently caught up in the spirit of my quest, Chaplin called me back the next day. "I have some more for you. Dundy County, Nebraska — that's on the fortieth parallel. They've got Ward Bond. Webster County, Nebraska — that's on the fortieth parallel. They've got Cy Young. And St. Francis, Kansas — that's where Ron Evans, the astronaut, is from."

—◆◇◆—

Before long the fortieth parallel was running into the high country. In Meeker, Colorado (1,800), Iva Kendall answered the phone at the White River Museum. "Kenneth Sanderson, who used the stage name Buddy Roosevelt, was born here and lived here," she said. I learned that Buddy Roosevelt was, among other things, Rudolf Valentino's double in *The Sheik,* and that his last film was *The Man Who Shot Liberty Valance.* Farther west, over into Utah, a young librarian answered the phone at the Payson City (10,000) Library. "This is so embarrassing," she said. "The only names that come to mind are Ron and Dan Lafferty. They're from Payson, and they got a lot of attention a few years ago when they murdered their sister-in-law and her daughter. It had to do with polygamy. They're in prison now, and one of them is on death row." The young librarian's supervisor called me the next day. "I can't believe all she could think of were the Laffertys. Maybe you could use Lewis Feild instead." Feild was the World Champion All-Around Cowboy in 1985, 1986, and 1987.

The Medicine Bow Mountains, the Park Range, the Sawatch Mountains, the Elk Mountains, the Great Salt Lake Desert — these were behind me now. In Fallon, Nevada (6,400), Bunny Corkill was on duty at the Churchill County Museum. I learned that Fallon was the home of Lieutenant Commander Bruce Van Voorhis, who fought in the Second World War and posthumously became Nevada's only Congressional Medal of Honor winner, and of Georgie Sicking, the "cowgirl poet" and the first Nevadan to be inducted into the Cowgirl Hall of Fame.

On to California. The first stop was Oroville (10,600). According to James Lenhoff, of the Butte County Historical Society, Erle Stanley Gardner, the author of the Perry Mason novels, lived in Oroville as a boy, and the actor Rod Taylor had a home there. Oroville, I learned, is also where Freda Ehmann developed a successful method for canning olives, allowing them to be marketed commercially. Alberta Guiver, the tour manager and manager of the gift shop at the Ehmann Home, said, "When she died, Ehmann had an obituary published in the 'Milestones' section of *Time* magazine." My last two stops were Red Bluff (11,500), where Leo Gorcey, of *The Bowery Boys* series, spent his final years, and Willits (4,000), where Black Bart, the stagecoach robber who left doggerel at the scene of his crimes, lived for much of his life. After completing a prison term, Black Bart was asked by a reporter whether he would continue to write poetry. "Young man," he said, "didn't you just hear me say I will commit no more crimes?"

The fortieth parallel descends from California's Coastal Range and enters the Pacific Ocean at an uninhabited spot south of a promontory known as Point Delgada. The waters are rich in marine life. On a hunch I called the Scripps Institution of Oceanography and asked the question I had been asking everyone else. A spokesman said, "Television's Flipper, the dolphin, and Disney's Sammy, the Way-Out Seal, were both captured off Point Delgada, and probably were born in the vicinity."

—◆◇◆—

No, that's a lie. I don't know where Flipper and Sammy came from. But the other stuff is all true. If you have been keeping a rough tally, as I have, you will have discovered that the people most likely to be local heroes across the land are, in this order, people in the movie business, writers (including cowperson poets), sports figures and people who have killed other people with guns (a tie), people in the music business, inventors and generals (a tie), and men of the cloth. Make of that what you will. No place that I called, however, was utterly bereft of distinction, or of pride.

Luck? Coincidence? A few days after completing my survey, I was looking at a map and noticed that the one hundredth meridian neatly bisects the country from north to south. I picked up the phone and called the local newspaper in Rugby, North Dakota (3,400), which is one of the northernmost U.S. towns astride the hundredth meridian. The receptionist at the *Pierce County Tribune* heard me out, mentioned in passing that Rugby lay at the exact geographical center of North America, and then put me through to the editor and publisher of the newspaper, Mark Carlson. Carlson didn't mince words. "Rugby," he said, "was the home of the florist N. P. Lindberg, who helped think up the slogan 'Say it with flowers' for FTD. That would have been in about 1910."

As I said, I haven't found Nowheresville yet. But I must admit, at times I've felt awfully close.

II

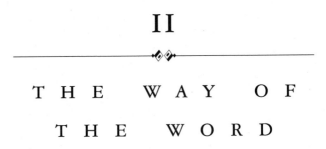

THE WAY OF THE WORD

The Big Nine

—◈◈—

A FOOTNOTE I came across not long ago in Robert Chapman's *New Dictionary of American Slang* contained a provocative reference to a study published in 1923 by the lexicographer G. H. McKnight. McKnight was interested in knowing which English words are used most commonly in conversation and how often the most commonly used English words occur. He eventually satisfied himself that out of some six hundred thousand living words in the language and a few hundred thousand more on various kinds of life support, a mere forty-three account for half the words actually uttered, and a mere nine account for fully a quarter of all spoken words. McKnight's Big Nine are *and, be, have, it, of, the, to, will,* and *you,* and the phenomenon he found at work in spoken English has been found, by other word frequency studies, in the English used in telephone conversations and in written English of all kinds.

This is the kind of preposterous scientific claim that fairly cries out for independent scrutiny, so I pulled down from the shelves and out of the drawers and off the refrigerator a selection of English-language texts: the Mayflower Compact, "Jabberwocky," Spiro Agnew's letter of resignation, the introduction to Internal Revenue Service Publication 920 ("Explanation of the Tax Reform Act of 1986 for Individuals"), the Boy Scout Oath, "The Marines' Hymn," the *Miranda* rights, which must be read to a suspect, a weekday example of the "Wizard of Id" comic strip, a section ("Flooded Engine") chosen at random from the owner's manual for a 1987 Colt Vista, a definition (for *egestion*) chosen at random from Samuel Johnson's *Dictionary,* a recipe (for gratin de homard et pâtes aux légumes) chosen at random from *The Ritz-Carlton Cookbook,* the first five verses of Saint Paul's epistle to the Galatians, Mikhail Gorbachev's remarks upon arriving at the White House during his first state visit, and the first question asked of the nominee by Edward Kennedy during the Senate Judiciary Committee's hearings in the matter of Robert Bork. These I subjected to an exhaustive and methodical investigation, in a spirit of cool skepticism, only to discover after many hours that McKnight's calculations are astonishingly accurate. To be specific, the percentages compiled by the Big Nine in the texts I examined are 29.7, 23.0, 33.3, 24.6, 25.0, 35.4, 32.1, 21.4, 25.0, 33.3, 26.9, 23.2, 24.6, and 25.7. The overall average is 27.4.

There are some unsurprising things about this group (the absence of *please* and *thank you,* for example) and some surprising and even heartening ones (the absence of *I*), but what has impressed me most about the Big Nine is how potent they are in the company of strangers and how helpless and insubstantial when left to themselves. To be sure, some of these words see each other socially — *to* and *be, of* and *the* — but if all nine were left alone in a room, they wouldn't know what to make of the occasion. I tried composing a thought using only the Big Nine and using each word only once, and could not, unless you don't regard as cheating this possible colloquy from the Watergate transcripts:

N: "You will be [garbled] of [garbled]."
H: "It [expletive deleted]."
N: "And the . . . ?"
H: "Have to [laughter]."

Yet even in the pained, awkward silence of their gathering the Big Nine cannot hide the potential for significant expression. Insubstantial they may be — there is not a noun among them — but they manage nonetheless to touch on a wide swath of reality: existence *(be)*, things *(it)*, others *(you)*, possessions *(of)*, the past *(have)*, the future *(will)*, and the urge to make lists *(and)*. They are enabling words — cajolers, enhancers, connectors — willing to help keep a conversation going but unable to start one or to suggest a subject. It is possible to speak profoundly without them — "I think, therefore I am" — but not for any length of time.

I admire McKnight's Big Nine for their economy and efficiency, but I admire them more for their steadfastness. It is hard to imagine how the constitution of this select group could change substantially. On the surface of the language, words are free to come and go. Changes in spelling and usage shape the terrain in ways both pleasant and malign. From time to time an especially noxious aberration will send shock waves deep into the mantle. But the Big Nine represent an unassailable core, a place where words will always be stable and pure, even if they are also mute.

No More Laissez-Faire

—◆◆—

L I N G U I S T I C

P R O T E C T I O N I S M

WHEN IT COMES to the circulation of words around the globe, I consider myself sympathetic to the forces of free trade. If members of a language community other than my own come up with a way of saying something better or more concisely than it has ever been said before — come up with the *mot juste* — then it is to the benefit of all of us that the new word or phrase acquire broader currency. A few years ago a collection of serviceable coinages was published under the title *They Have a Word for It*. It included, for example, the New Guinean word *mokita*, which refers to "truth everybody knows but nobody speaks," and the German word *Treppenwitz*, meaning a "clever remark that comes to mind when it is too late to utter it." Words like these are valuable commodities, and there is no reason to confine them to one small patch of geography.

In good free-market fashion, people pick up words from foreign languages when it's useful or necessary to do so — as, for example, when new products or concepts arrive with foreign names attached to them. Needless to say, some languages appear on the scene and contribute almost nothing. The Visigoths swept through Spain in the fifth century A.D. and ruled the peninsula for well over two centuries; hardly a single word of the Visigothic tongue survives in Spain. In contrast, languages such as Latin and English have sent useful words by the thousands to foreign shores.

No one regulates all this activity. No one needs to; a natural dynamism is at work. And though it can be held at bay by the outright censorship of publishing and broadcasting, the trade in words is otherwise not greatly susceptible to manipulation or control. Millions of dollars' worth of advertising by Volkswagen was unequal to the task of making *Fahrvergnügen* a word that Americans felt they really needed. By the same token, *samizdat, sushi,* and *blitzkrieg* caught on fast, and it is hard to imagine that they could ever be dislodged by substitutes. The system of free trade in words has been in place since the dawn of time, and people almost everywhere, even in Japan, rightly see it as a robust manifestation of human creativity.

And then there are the French. Although they have been the happy beneficiaries of a free-trade regime on the part of other nations — especially during the eighteenth and nineteenth centuries, when their language was the language of diplomacy and penetrated jungle and tundra, prairie and steppe — the French have always returned the favor by attempting to seal the linguistic border. Their first great enemy was Latin. Next came Italian and German. Then, a few centuries ago, the French began to worry about *contamination* (their term) by English.

The influx of English words into French was being denounced as early as 1757, by Fougeret de Monbron in his book *Préservatif contre l'anglomanie.* In our own time the threat posed by English was memorably described by Réné Étiemble in his book *Parlez-vous franglais?,* and ever since its publication, in 1964, complaints about the contamination of French by such words as *le weekend, le cash flow,* and *le sandwich* have been a staple of public commentary in France. As one element of France's bid for linguistic autarky, a commission has been established to come up with French equivalents for intrusive foreign words (for instance, *le gros-porteur* instead of *le jumbo jet*). Despite such official measures, from time to time the level of concern assumes crisis proportions, and the world looks on as the French noisily undergo ritual purification.

The French have been in a purifying mood since the 1990s began, owing in part to nervousness about the consequences for their language of a somewhat more united Europe. Characteristically, they have indulged their protectionist impulses. During the summer of 1992 a joint session of the French Parliament was convened at the Palace of Versailles in order to add the following sentence to France's constitution: "The language of the republic is French." The sentence may seem innocuous, but it effectively reduces the status of English words that have wide currency in France to that of guest workers there. Shortly after this constitutional amendment was ratified, a group of three hundred French intellectuals issued a declaration that denounced the aural and visual presence of English in France. "We cannot accept this process of collective self-destruction," they wrote. The intellectuals criticized the growing number of "angloglots" in France and called for a stepped-up government campaign against "linguistic debasement."

It is perhaps going a little too far to say that the quickest way to make me change an opinion is to tell me that three hundred French intellectuals share it, but it does seem in this case that the French might benefit from a modest sense of perspective. Consider what English-speakers have had to put up with at the hands of French-speakers. Until the year 1066, English was an essentially Germanic tongue with roughly fifty or sixty thousand words. Then came the Battle of Hastings, and in its aftermath William of Normandy and his French-speaking retainers came to power in Britain. During the first three hundred years after Hastings, the kings of England were all speakers of French. So great was the cultural domination of French that relatively few documents from 1066 until the thirteenth century exist in English. When written English at last reappeared, in the form of Middle English, it had doubled in size since pre-Norman days, and almost all the new words were loan-words from French. Besides the many tens of thousands of French words that have been incorporated into English in anglicized form, countless French words and phrases have been incorporated without change, and are even deemed by some to have a certain cachet. The historical infusion of French into English is of far greater magnitude (and came about with far greater loss of life) than anything that happened in the other direction.

Yet despite all that, we speakers of English generally profess to be quite satisfied with our mongrel tongue. When reminded of what the Normans wrought, our reaction is likely to be *"C'est la vie."*

The time has come, I think, for the English-speaking world, and the United States in particular, to communicate to the French our desire for a more open frame of mind on their part. The way to do this is in effect to answer tariff barriers with tariff barriers.

To begin with, I would urge restaurants across the country to take a step that happens in any case to be long overdue: put an end to the practice of writing menus in French, which is the gastronomical equivalent of the Latin mass. This change should not apply merely to expensive French restaurants. Even lowly diners can be found with a soup *du jour* on the menu, and I hope that the owners will opt for the vernacular.

Translating our menus is probably not enough to produce a change of heart in a Régis Debray or a Eugene Ionesco, so I would next ask English-speakers to begin weeding French words and phrases from their vocabulary. At a minimum, I would suggest eliminating the following ten terms, all of which keep an exceedingly high profile: *avant-garde, savoir-faire, tour de force, de rigueur, fait accompli, déjà vu, lèse majesté, raison d'être, belles lettres,* and *laissez-faire.* In addition, there are a number of French phrases — *je ne sais quoi, comme ci comme ça, quelque chose, quel dommage* — with which people of a certain type seed their conversation, and these, too, should be abandoned. For good measure I would add to the list of proscriptions certain widely quoted French epigrams: the irresponsible *Après moi, le déluge;* the totalitarian *L'état, c'est moi;* the fatalistic *Plus ça change, plus c'est la même chose.*

If this ban on imports had no effect, I would then feel compelled to take the fight to the French homeland. To begin with, I would ask English-speaking visitors to the cathedral town of Rheims to stop trying to pronounce the town's name correctly — that is, trying to make it sound like something between a clearing of the throat and a sinus attack. As we all know, the French have a special organ in their noses that makes such pronunciations effortless, but very few English-speakers are so equipped. Speakers of English should therefore do what comes naturally and in a loud voice always refer to Rheims as "Reems." Similarly, on visits to the Louvre ("Loov"), and especially when guards are standing close by, English-speaking visitors should not try to pronounce the name of the artist Ingres the way the French do — as if a couple of fingers had been stuck down their throats — but instead employ a straightforward "Ingress." With nine million English-speaking tourists visiting France every year, it shouldn't take more than a few summers before the French get the message.

Yet they may not, and it is for this remote eventuality that we must reserve a final weapon. I am reluctant to use it; France and the United States are historic allies. But if protectionist attitudes persist, we should press ahead with a selective trade embargo. Specifically, English-speaking countries should ban the export to France of any product whose name the French deem offensive. The embargo might take effect in stages, with, say, an initial ban on the export of *les blue jeans, les Big Macs,* and recordings of *le rock and roll.* In the absence of a prompt change of attitude on the part of the French, the embargo could rapidly be expanded.

Needless to say, I hope it does not come to this. I look forward to the day, perhaps not too far distant, when a French-speaker confronted by linguistic contamination in a French magazine or newspaper can turn to a friend and say, with a shrug of Gallic indifference, "That's life."

Huiswants Es

—◆◇◆—

S A Y I N G   H E L L O

I N   H I T T I T E

FIVE TIMES a year the U.S. government's National Endowment for the Humanities publishes a list of which institutions have received how much money for what scholarly purposes. As soon as it arrives, I look first under the heading "Language & Linguistics" to see if any new dictionary-of-dead-language projects have received a green light or if any of the old dead-language standbys have received extensions of support. Something along those lines is almost always there. For example, one list that arrived a short time ago announced new funding for *The Assyrian Dictionary,* a project that scholars at the University of Chicago have been working on since the 1920s. The endowment has also helped to finance work on the *Thesaurus Linguae Graecae, The Sumerian Dictionary, The Comprehensive Aramaic Lexicon, A Dictionary of Jewish Babylonian Aramaic, A Dictionary of Jewish Palestinian Aramaic,* the *Demotic Egyptian Dictionary,* and *The Hittite Dictionary,* and a dozen more such efforts are under way. At least insofar as scholarly attention is concerned, there has never been a better time to be a dead language.

Necrolexicography, as the making of dictionaries of dead languages has been good-naturedly called, has always struck me as being about as seductive a scholarly endeavor as can be. It has, to begin with, a certain stodgy romance. It brings the word *lucubration* naturally to mind, with all its pleasing associations: cracked leather bindings, a whiff of tallow under the eaves, a chill cobalt night beyond the leaded panes. The work partakes of a long and venerable tradition, stretching back at least a century and a half. It is essential to the study of history. It is also that great rarity, an academic undertaking of distinguished pedigree that is multicultural to its very core, being concerned by definition with diverse peoples. Those peoples, moreover, are usually no longer around to complain. Disputes do arise, but they tend to be over issues that are technical, sort of fun, and unlikely to do major harm to the human race; for example, over whether one can differentiate a distinct Middle Hittite, in addition to Old and New Hittite. Finally, to have one's name associated with the definitive dictionary of a dead language guarantees one a measure of immortality roughly equivalent to that which the dictionary has given the language itself.

Had it been my lot to labor in academe, a career devoted to fashioning a dictionary of Moabite or Philistine would probably have been irresistible. And whenever I come upon the roster of newly funded ventures into dead languages, I feel a momentary pang of opportunity forgone.

That is no doubt why, after seeing the latest list, I resolved to look into necrolexicography a little further, a search that eventually led to several amiable conversations with Professor Harry Hoffner, at the University of Chicago's Oriental Institute. Hoffner directs the team that since 1976 has been laboring to produce a dictionary of Hittite, a language in which written records dating from about 1750 B.C. to about 1200 B.C. exist in the form of cuneiform on clay tablets. The Hittites, as you may remember from high school history or Sunday school, lived in what is now Turkey. Their military prowess was legendary, enhanced, some sources say, by an advanced form of chariot. I have always had a fond regard for the Hittites. They built one of the great ancient civilizations, but their accomplishments, unlike those of other

Near Eastern cultures, have yet to be immortalized in English fable and verse. In Byron's poem it is an Assyrian, not a Hittite, who "came down like the wolf on the fold." (As Hoffner reminded me when we spoke, for all their might the Hittites generally preferred diplomacy to force of arms — "and I am not being a Hittite chauvinist," he hastened to add.)

The Chicago project, which aims to produce what Hoffner calls "the OED of Hittite," with many textual citations for every known word, is actually one of two Hittite dictionaries in the making, the other being the product of a German team in Munich. The Munich and Chicago scholars are divided on various issues, mostly having to do with how to date the writing on clay tablets (*is* there a Middle Hittite, and if so, which texts are written in it?), so the projects proceed independently. The Munich team started with Hittite words that, when rendered phonetically in Roman script, begin with the letter *A*. So as not to give the impression that it was plowing planted ground, the Chicago team, which started its work later, began with the letter *L*. It has done *M*, *N*, and *P*, and has ahead of it *S*, *T*, *U*, *W*, and *Z* (there is no *O*, *Q*, *V*, *X*, or *Y* in Hittite, and no words begin with *R*), plus, eventually, the front end of the alphabet — *A*, *E*, *H*, *I*, and *K* (there is no *F* or *J* in Hittite; *B* words fall under *P*, *C* and *G* words under *K*, and *D* words under *T*).

Hittite is an important language, and there is a lot of it to work with: some thirty thousand clay tablets or fragments of tablets have survived, most of them from literary archives uncovered at the Hittite capital, Hattusha, beginning in 1906. The language remained undeciphered until 1915, when a Czech Assyriologist, Bedrich Hrozný, showed that Hittite was not a member of the same language family as Assyrian and Babylonian, even though it was written in the same cuneiform script. Hittite turned out to be an Indo-European language, not a Semitic one, and indeed it belongs to the oldest known branch of Indo-European, the language family of which English is a member. Hrozný and others worked out the basics — how the verbs and nouns worked, what the pronouns were — and over the years scholars compiled word lists and glossaries. By the 1970s enough was known to make possible a full-fledged dictionary. The Chicago project was launched by Hoffner and his colleague Hans Gustav Güterbock, who is now in his eighties and continues to be involved in its affairs.

I asked Hoffner if he could explain some of the intricacies of his work. "The Hittites," he said, "are so remote in time and place that there are lots of words whose meanings we still don't know, especially words for things like trees, bushes, fruits, and animals. What sometimes saves us is that in cuneiform the Hittites often made use of Babylonian symbols, which they employed as a kind of shorthand. We often have several copies of the same text — like having several editions of *Alice in Wonderland,* say — where one copy of the text will be entirely in Hittite and another will have all these Babylonian symbols in it in various places. So it works like a Rosetta Stone."

By this means Hoffner himself, some ten years ago, discovered the Hittite word for "brother." He had come across the phrase "brothers having the same father," in which the Hittite term for father, *pappa,* was combined with a Babylonian symbol for "brothers." "I just thought I'd look at all the *pappas* on our cards to see which ones had other Hittite elements attached, and I eventually came upon *pappanegnesh.* I tried translating the singular noun *negna-* as 'brother' in other citations we had, and it worked. I made the discovery just in time to include *negna-* in the N volume."

Hoffner offered another example of the sort of chance encounter that can lead to a sudden connection. A similarity had long been noticed between two Hittite words — *armizzi,* which means "bridge," and *armizziyah,* which means "to divulge." Morphologically, the relatedness seemed indisputable. But how might the two meanings be linked? Professor Güterbock found the probable answer one day when he happened upon this epigram in a Hittite text: "The tongue is a bridge."

There is a lot of wordplay in Hittite texts. Some of it shows up in words for alcoholic beverages. One drink was called *walhi,* a name that seems to be related to the verb meaning "to hit hard." Another drink was called *marnuwan,* a name that seems to be related to the verb meaning "to disappear." Hoffner said, "We've even found a Hittite magic ritual in which, after a patient is given *marnuwan* to drink, the magician uses this verb to command the patient's ills to go away."

Was there anything else Hoffner found particularly fetching about Hittite? "Well," he said, "the word the Hittites used for the verb 'to put on,' as in 'to put on an article of clothing,' was different for each garment." He thought for a moment. "I've also always liked the way the Hittites said hello. The standard form of greeting was *Huiswants es,* which means 'Be alive.'"

I asked Hoffner how the Hittites said goodbye. He could not tell me. No recovered text, he said, contains a situation in which anyone needs to say it. "Maybe," he added, "as in Hebrew, they just said hello again."

There is something affecting about even a brief encounter with a once-living language. Partly, I suppose, this is because such encounters allow us to see familiar human traits turn up convincingly in strange contexts. Partly, too, it is because they remind us that when these dead languages were spoken, people felt themselves to be living as much in the present as we do now. We may soon be made more aware of the reasons, whatever they are.

I mentioned that there has never been a better time to be a dead language. Sadly, there has also never been a better time to become one. It has been estimated that more than six thousand languages are spoken in the world today. Of these, about half are now spoken by fewer than five thousand people. As many as a thousand languages are classified by linguists as dying or moribund, the helpless victims of cultural engulfment. Some of these languages may have just entered the terminal phase, the chief symptom of which is that they are no longer being taught to children. Others are moments from death, with only a handful of speakers left. Among the worst-hit languages are those of the native peoples of the New World. Klallam and Gros Ventre, for example, are down to fewer than twenty speakers each. Mandan is down to six. Tolowa is down to four or five. Indigenous languages in Australia have also been dying off rapidly. The process is occurring everywhere. In the Caucasus, a language called Ubykh, which is renowned for being the language with the most consonants (about eighty), has one remaining speaker.

Some three thousand years elapsed between the death of Hittite and the birth of a Hittite dictionary project. Nowadays, the interval between death and dictionary is typically a small fraction of that length, and the chronology is sometimes even reversed; for today's threatened languages, dictionary projects are desperately coming to life a decade or two before the language's projected demise. A Klallam dictionary has been in the making for some years (and is supported in part by the National Endowment for the Humanities). So has a Gros Ventre dictionary. So have a number of others. Hundreds of languages, of course, are destined simply to disappear, having been committed neither to writing nor to tape. The world's languages are as endangered as the world's species — indeed, in terms of percentage loss, language is in more desperate straits.

For such languages as can be caught, the most likely route to survival is captivity. An extinct language trapped in the amber of a dictionary may be a poignant thing to behold, yet it enjoys an incomparable advantage over an extinct plant or animal: it has not in fact wholly died. The iguanodon, the Steller's sea cow, the Tasmanian tiger, the dodo — they are gone, never to reappear. But a language, no matter how long in suspended animation, can again partake of life and resume its evolution anytime people decide to speak it. I'm not sure whether it was an invitation, but at one point in our conversation Professor Hoffner said, "You know, Hittite is actually easier to learn than Latin or Greek."

Fortunately, the survival of Hittite and other dead languages depends not on me but on the necrolexicographers who quietly tend the embers. I don't know if they have a motto, but *Huiswants es* would do just fine.

"To Be" in Their Bonnets

—◆◇◆—

A M A T T E R O F

S E M A N T I C S

RECENTLY I OPENED UP an issue (Volume 48, Number 2) of *Et cetera,* the quarterly journal of the International Society for General Semantics, and within a few minutes of doing so got a bit of a surprise. The surprise came from an article by Emory Menefee, a former president of the ISGS, which bluntly calls into question attempts by many society members to promote something called E-Prime, a form of English that has for years ranked extremely high among the interests of the general-semantics community. Advocates of E-Prime, for reasons that I'll come to, favor the elimination in English of every form of the verb *to be* — *be, been, is, am, are, was, were, 'm, 's, 're,* and all the rest. They not only promote E-Prime as a theoretical proposition but also try in daily life to erase *to be* and its inflections from everything they write. The most committed advocates use E-Prime even when they talk. Given all this, to see the E-Prime endeavor criticized in an official organ — to see that endeavor, indeed, termed "quixotic" — naturally raised an eyebrow. When I queried the International Society for General Semantics about the matter, the executive director, Paul Dennithorne Johnston, assured me that the society never did and does not now regard E-Prime as tantamount to some sort of party line. Well, fine. But it has strong support among the *nomenklatura,* and I do not expect them to hold their peace.

General semantics originated in the work of a Polish engineer, Count Alfred Korzybski, who first spelled out his ideas about language and other symbolic structures in 1933 in his book *Science and Sanity.* Korzybski had come to the United States in 1915 and eventually became a citizen. In 1938 he established the Institute of General Semantics in Chicago. The institute moved to Lime Rock, Connecticut, late in 1946. (The field has two journals. In 1943 a student of Korzybski's, the noted semanticist and one-term U.S. senator S. I. Hayakawa, founded *Et cetera,* which currently has about 2,500 subscribers. Korzybski's associate M. Kendig founded the *General Semantics Bulletin* in 1950.)

Explanations of general semantics can become pretty elaborate pretty fast, but the basic idea sounds simple enough. Most of us think of language as something that reflects reality or at least allows us to express our perceptions of reality. Without denying this, general semanticists believe that the very structure of language can influence or distort our perceptions, and they contend that a failure to observe the many ways in which language can do this results in an inability to apprehend the meaning not only of other people's words but of our own as well. This, of course, causes problems, the size of which can range from the most minor misunderstanding to complete metaphysical disarray, and the problems, naturally, spill over into the realm of behavior. Korzybski himself took a grave view of the actual and potential consequences of "semantic damage." Semanticists observe, tellingly, that the carnage of the First World War powerfully catalyzed Korzybski's thinking.

General semantics over the years has taken up a diverse array of subjects touching on language — for example, double-speak, logic, newspaper headlines, nonverbal communication, objectivity, cultural relativism, euphemism, metaphor — but through it all the verb *to be* has remained a core of concern. That many people in the field, including Korzybski, would zero in on this verb strikes one in retrospect as entirely predictable; after all, philosophers called attention to its problematic character at least as early as the seventeenth century, and their uneasiness had not let up by the twentieth. "The little word *is* has its tragedies," George Santayana wrote in 1923, in a passage that general semanticists quote frequently and fondly.

> It names and identifies different things with the greatest innocence; and yet no two are ever identical, and if therein lies the charm of wedding them and calling them one, therein too lies the danger. Whenever I use the word *is,* except in sheer tautology, I deeply misuse it; and when I discover my error, the world seems to fall asunder.

Santayana's complaint had to do with locutions like "Mary is a woman" and "Mary is cold," in which the verb *is* implies the tight coupling of equivalent things, whereas in fact in the first instance it joins nouns that have different levels of abstraction and in the second it joins a noun to an adjective that neither completely nor permanently qualifies it. Transgressions like these may seem trivial, but in fact they pose fundamental problems of logic, and they greatly bother critical thinkers.

To these sins of the verb *to be* semanticists have added many others. For example, the verb makes possible the widespread use of the passive voice, conditioning us to accept detours around crucial issues of causality ("Mistakes were made"). It makes possible the raising of unanswerable, because hopelessly formulated, questions ("What is truth?"). It makes possible, too, the construction of a variety of phrases ("As is well known . . .") that casually sweep reasoning under a rug. One also finds the verb *to be* pressed into service on behalf of stereotypical labeling ("Scotsmen are stingy") and overbroad existential generalization ("I'm just no good"). These issues aside, semanticists say, the verb *to be,* broadly speaking, imputes an Aristotelian neatness, rigidity, and permanence to the world around us and to the relationships among all the things in it — conditions that rarely have any basis in a dynamic reality.

Although Korzybski and others fashioned an indictment of *to be* relatively early in the history of general semantics, the idea of actually getting rid of the verb altogether dates back only to the late 1940s, when it occurred to D. David Bourland, Jr., at that time a Korzybski fellow at Lime Rock. Bourland first used his writing system, which he eventually called E-Prime (E'), in an article, "Introduction to a Structural Calculus: A Postulational Statement of Alfred Korzybski's Non-Aristotelian Linguistic System," that appeared without fanfare in the *General Semantics Bulletin* in 1952. (He derived the term "E-Prime" from the equation $E'=E-e$, where E represents standard English and e represents the inflected forms of *to be*.) Bourland would later recall that writing this article left him with "an intermittent, but severe, headache which lasted for about a week." Strange as it may seem, a piece of text in polished E-Prime does not necessarily alert readers to the E-Prime aspect of its character, and Bourland continued to use E-Prime, unnoticed by the outside world, in his work. Indeed, he deliberately took no steps to call wide attention to how he wrote, lest, as he also recalled, "I become regarded as some kind of nut." Eventually, though, a few close friends prevailed upon Bourland to go public, which in a manner of speaking he did, in 1965, with another article in the *General Semantics Bulletin,* this one titled "A Linguistic Note: Writing in E-Prime." Since then E-Prime in its written form has acquired several dozen practitioners within the general-semantics community.

As for its oral form, those familiar with E-Prime point to an independent research scientist in Oregon named E. W. Kellogg III as perhaps America's most accomplished E-Prime speaker (the competition consists of three or four other people, including David Bourland), and I decided to give Kellogg a call. I expected to hear someone speaking in a slow and considered manner, as if picking his way uncertainly through a linguistic swamp, but he talked briskly and with what sounded like supreme self-confidence. Yes, he said, he halted a lot when he first started speaking E-Prime, in 1978, and a lot of sentences ended abruptly in the middle when he could see himself running into an *is*. At times he lapsed into a kind of pidgin E-Prime. The transition, in short, took some work. "I had to cope with all that backlog of *is*-pattern English," he explained. "And I had to do it in real time." But Kellogg got the hang of it stylistically after a year or so, and he now strives in his speech (as he and others also do in writing) to effect further refinements. These include ridding his vocabulary of instances of absolutism (for example, such words as *always* and *ever*, which imply immutability) and of many nouns made out of verbs (in particular those with a *-tion* ending, such as *visualization* and *procrastination*, which freeze ongoing processes into static events). Kellogg also hopes to reduce his reliance on *have*, which quite often can substitute for *is*, and on other crutches, like *appear* and *seem*. "I aim at a more phenomenological ideal," he said. "I try to move toward a language that communicates the territory of my experience to myself and others as clearly and accurately as possible." As we spoke, Kellogg's voice at times gathered a certain momentum, clipped and commanding, comfortable in its fluency. As a salesman for E-Prime, he excelled.

Now back to Emory Menefee, who in his *Et cetera* article makes several arguments against E-Prime and in favor of what he calls E-Choice (a term that, as he good-naturedly acknowledges, "arose from the strained similarity between the term E-Prime and a USDA meat grade"). For one thing, Menefee notes, most general semanticists consider certain uses of *to be* unobjectionable — for example, as an auxiliary verb, or to convey the fact of existence, or to create metaphors. Why throw these uses out? (E-Prime advocates, in reply, make an argument for total abstinence similar to the ones heard with respect to smoking or drinking.) Moreover, Menefee goes on, most of the problems caused by the misuse of *to be* can occur in E-Prime as well, especially if a speaker hasn't internalized all the underlying logic involved; the bloody-minded human cortex can easily work its way around a little obstacle like the proscription of a few words. And in any event, Menefee observes, in the real world E-Prime can never hope to achieve a status other than its present one — as the plaything of a handful of enthusiasts. Menefee concedes, in the end, only that E-Prime may perhaps serve usefully as a "pedagogic tool to force extreme attention on the verb 'to be.'"

Anyone wishing to explore the E-Prime issue further can turn to *Et cetera* itself and to a collection of essays, titled *To Be or Not,* published by the ISGS, in San Francisco. I myself, having seen the intensity that general semanticists can bring to their work, have no intention of stepping cavalierly into the maw of this debate. Volume 48, Number 3, of *Et cetera* will, I expect, feature bloody reprisals. And yet, having used E-Prime for nine paragraphs now, I would venture to pray that the parties involved could find common ground on one point. Whether E-Prime deserves to become more or no more than a pedagogic tool, surely we can all hope that it might become *at least* a pedagogic tool. Almost all of us tend to overuse *to be*. E-Prime shows how we overuse it. It forces one relentlessly to confront sloppiness, laziness, fuzziness, blandness, imprecision, simplistic generalization, and a half-dozen other all too frequent characteristics of casual prose. As a self-administered exercise, this single restraint on style, with all the discomfort that may ensue, offers more real insight in an afternoon than one could gain from a year's worth of spoken precepts.

And the cost? In my case, a mere headache, severe but intermittent. I have reason to believe it will last about a week.

"Hey, Let Me Outta Here!"

VENTRILOQUISTS

AND THEIR VOICES

WHEN I FIRST MET Ollie, he was beside himself, with his head lying alongside his torso in a wooden box. Jeff Dunham gently lifted the pieces out and helped Ollie pull himself together. When he was seated on Dunham's knee, Ollie opened his eyes, looked at me, furrowed his brow, recoiled, and turned his head to the familiar face on his right.

"Who the heck is that?" he asked Dunham.

Dunham made the introduction, but Ollie would have none of it. "Do you have any idea what time it is?"

Ollie glowered, and his upper lip curled back in a menacing sneer. Dunham handed him to me and said, "Be careful." I cradled Ollie on my lap and inserted my right hand into his thoracic cavity. The anatomy was unfamiliar, but I depressed one lever and then another and then a third. Ollie turned his head, dropped his jaw, and winked. A moment later his nose lit up bright red. His left eyebrow ascended. He sneered again. I handed Ollie back, and he seemed relieved.

"That was awful," he said to Dunham. "Don't ever let him near me again."

Dunham soothed the little fellow and then returned him to his box. "I'm sorry about that," he said to me. "Ollie can be temperamental."

In Ollie's defense, I should note that it *was* late — around midnight on the last day of the International Ventriloquist Con-VENTion (the curious orthography derives from the term that "vents" use for one another), which is held every year at midsummer in Fort Mitchell, Kentucky, a suburb of Cincinnati, Ohio. Dunham, Ollie's current owner and a rising young ventriloquist, was the chairman of the convention, and he hadn't had much free time. I had wanted to see and hold Ollie because he is one of the few figures (vents tend to prefer this term to *dummies,* but they use both) made by the McElroy brothers, Glenn and George, that remain on active duty.

In the 1930s the McElroys produced a series of perhaps a hundred mechanical characters, each of which in the world of ventriloquism enjoys the status of a Stradivarius. During the Second World War, when supplies became scarce, they took jobs at Ivory Soap's Toilet Goods Model Shop, in Ivorydale, Ohio, and virtually stopped making figures for the rest of their careers (they are now retired). The head of a typical McElroy figure was molded in plastic wood and painted with subtlety and skill. Features that had to be especially pliable — the eyelids, the retractable lips — were fashioned from leather or chamois and grafted imperceptibly onto the head. The mechanical works inside Ollie, which Jeff Dunham exposed by removing a plate in the cranium, resemble a heaping bowl of metallic pasta; they make possible some fourteen movements of the face and head. The wiring, fashioned largely from bicycle spokes, trails down the metal spine upon which the head is impaled to a set of levers that resemble typewriter keys, and it is essentially by typing that a ventriloquist manipulates a McElroy figure. A few days before I met Ollie face to face, I had seen how Dunham, in performance, made Ollie come alive. Every vent is at home with his own "headstick"; when I tried to manipulate Ollie myself, it was like driving a standard-transmission car with fourteen stick shifts. "Ollie takes some getting used to," Dunham said. "He's more complex than all but a handful of figures. It is such a privilege to work with him."

The world of which Dunham and Ollie are a part was foreign to me until I accepted an invitation to attend the fourteenth annual ventriloquists' convention and spent some time in the company of four hundred people who, in the words of one vent, "like to talk to themselves and play with dolls." I was unaware before arriving that ventriloquism, like tap dancing and other vaudevillian arts, is enjoying a considerable popular revival. I had never given more than a passing thought to the vocal, manipulative, and engineering skills that the ventriloquist's illusion requires. And I did not realize the extent to which ventriloquism, like puppetry in general, has swept through evangelical Christianity and become a mainstay of modern ministry.

Three days and nights in Fort Mitchell changed all that. I met a half-dozen of the finest ventriloquists in the world. I saw several dozen performances. I spoke to people who make figures and learned some of the basics of their craft. I came home with the makings of a figure of my own, and with the desire to attend another convention when the memory of my initial immersion begins to dim. It hasn't yet.

—◆◇◆—

On the night before the opening of the convention there was a performance, which the public could attend for a dollar or two, by Ronn Lucas, one of the most innovative ventriloquists working today. Every seat in front of the stage at the Drawbridge Inn in Fort Mitchell, where the convention is always held, seemed to be occupied by someone talking to someone else on his or her lap. In some cases both parties to a conversation were sentient beings, but from the rear of the hall it was hard to tell the children from the dummies.

When Ronn Lucas came out with the figure for which he is most widely known, Buffalo Billy, I realized that I had seen him once with Johnny Carson on the *Tonight Show*. Lucas is young, good-looking, and clean-cut in a midwestern sort of way. He had just gotten married, he told the audience, despite his fiancée's concern that his lips wouldn't move. Lucas eased gently into the kind of routine that is familiar to anyone who has ever seen a ventriloquist, in which the smart-alecky dummy takes on the increasingly bewildered vent. He demonstrated his command of the distant voice (the voice that seems to come from another part of the room or over the telephone) and the muffled voice (the voice that seems to come from inside a trunk or suitcase). Gradually Lucas added new dimensions to his act. In one routine he blew up a balloon while Buffalo Billy sang the ABC song. In another Billy held a figure in his lap and seemed himself to be a ventriloquist, creating an ever-shifting web of real and illusory relationships. Lucas then abandoned his figures and performed for a while with nothing but a sock that he wore on his hand. He discarded the sock and launched into a skit in which the microphone became his interlocutor, its voice tinny and electric and at times seemingly disturbed by interference. Before long the microphone, too, was abandoned, and Lucas performed what can only be described as a ballet, in which his bare hand danced to a strange music that the hand itself seemed to be producing. The music culminated in a high-pitched and steady whine, as if from a tuning fork, and it seemed to come from a spot Lucas pointed to on his palm. He turned the palm to the audience and the whine became louder. He turned the palm away and the whine became softer. He held his palm flat and the sound steadied for a moment, then began slowly to fade. Before the sound could fade away completely, Lucas abruptly closed his hand, and there was silence. The people in the hall made no move to applaud for five or six seconds, as if applause were too blunt and bestial a response to what they had just seen. I clearly wasn't the only one in the room whose rapture was tarnished by envy.

If a genie appeared and offered you three wishes, you probably wouldn't use one to become a ventriloquist. But if you happened to wake up one day with a ventriloquist's skills, you probably would admit that something wonderful had happened. Ventriloquism is a talent that almost no one would mind having. I remember advertisements in comic books for ventriloquism lessons which showed a big guy, maybe a sailor, carrying a trunk on his back, and from the trunk came the plaintive cry. "Hey, let me outta here!" A little kid with a devilish grin was shown standing nearby. I never clipped the coupon and sent in money, but the ad has always stuck in my mind, emblematic, perhaps, of a career path too early forsworn.

If I had followed that path, however, there would be a few things I could say about myself by now. I would probably be an alumnus of the Maher Ventriloquist Studios, which turns out as many as four hundred vents a year and which, incredibly, conducts all its classes by mail. I would have invested $1,000 or more in the figures I now used, which I would carry around in a trunk. I would have publicity photographs on my person at all times, and they would show me mugging for the camera with my dummy, wearing the expression you see in every picture of Willard Scott. I would be disliked by standup comics, who find distasteful the use of a prop and who also frequently bomb when they have to follow vents. I would wear Hawaiian shirts on inappropriate occasions. And no matter what kind of ventriloquist I was, I would show up at the International Ventriloquist ConVENTion at least once every couple of years, because going there is good for art and good for business.

The International Ventriloquist ConVENTion is on one level a professional meeting like any other. There are lectures and workshops, a business meeting and an awards banquet, an exhibition hall and a hospitality suite. And there is a lot of shop-

talk. Ventriloquism is a diverse endeavor with far-flung practitioners, and the convention is the one place where everyone can
catch up with what's happening in the profession. Nobody can
do better than guess at how many people work as professional
ventriloquists in the United States, but the number of people
coming to the convention increases every year. Keeping vents
supplied with dummies provides work for about fifteen small
businesses in this country. And ventriloquism, which nearly died
when vaudeville did, has moved into many new arenas.

Clinton Detweiler, who owns the Maher Ventriloquist Studios
and is the editor of the newsletter *Newsy Vents,* and who seems
to spend most of his spare time figuring out ways to incorporate
mouths that can open and close into plastic fruit and neckties
and watering cans and other items around the house, sat me
down one afternoon at the convention and drew a pie chart. "I
don't know how many vents altogether are in this pie," Detweiler said, "but if you had to divide them up percentagewise,
it would look something like this. About five percent would be
your standups, working in places like Atlantic City, Chicago,
and Las Vegas or on cruise ships. Another twenty percent do
mainly programs in schools — you know, for drug education
and that sort of thing. And another twenty percent are part-time
vents who do community-type shows and shows at parties. Maybe
ten percent are teachers or doctors or lawyers or psychologists
who use dummies in their work. And maybe five percent are
people in business who'll use a dummy for seminars and what-
not, and probably another five percent are vents in ways I
haven't thought of. We'll call that 'other.' Another twenty percent
are hobbyists. And then you have your gospel vents, who make
up at least a quarter of the pie and probably more, and that share
is growing." Detweiler looked down at the pie. "So that comes
to a hundred and ten percent. Well, there's some overlap, I guess."

A woman approached with a toy duck and asked Detweiler
if he could find a way to give it a working mouth, and he said
to leave it with him for a while and he'd see if he could rig one

up, maybe with a clothespin. When the woman left, Detweiler said, "I spend a lot of time in grocery stores looking for things I can put mouths on. Generally the cereal aisles and the detergent aisles are the best, but in fact you'll find things almost anywhere you look. That's my problem."

The dealers' room is the heart of the convention, where most of the socializing occurs, and I walked around it one night for several hours. Dummies of all kinds, old and new, lay out on tables: drunks, dogs, and dons, grandmothers and goons, sailors, leprechauns, bullies. There was a Vietnam veteran dummy in a wheelchair. The heads of many of the antique dummies were open to expose the works, and the cranial plates lay upturned beside the heads like ashtrays. Ventriloquists mingled among the stalls with their figures on their arms. The figures tended to greet one another in the aisles. Behind my back someone said, "That's the most beautiful ventriloquist's figure I've ever seen." Someone else said in reply, "Shari Lewis has the most beautiful ventriloquist's figure *I've* ever seen." Some dealers had small libraries for sale. The books bore titles like *Something Punny* and *Knock Em Dead* and *Conquering Stage Fright*. At Clinton Detweiler's table you could buy *Shredded Wit*, a book of jokes on cereal themes. One dealer showed me a collection of English music-hall routines. "If you really want a weird act, get one of these. It's all 'bloody' this and 'bloody' that." He was also selling Charlie McCarthy spoons from the 1930s and yellowing original scripts from *The Paul Winchell Show*. A dealer nearby was offering, for $200, a suit that had once been worn by Mortimer Snerd. Two seven-year-olds walked past me with dummies perched on their forearms. One of them said to the other, "So how long you been a vent?"

—◆◆—

The International Ventriloquist ConVENTion is held in Fort Mitchell because that is the home of the Vent Haven Museum, which houses the largest collection of ventriloquist's figures in the world. The museum was opened to the public (by appointment) in 1973, after the death of William Shakespeare Berger, who was a president of the Cambridge Tile Company, in Cincinnati, an amateur ventriloquist, and a collector of ventriloquial materials: not only figures and puppets but also books, photographs, scripts, recordings, films, and woodcarving tools. The museum was initially confined to Berger's red brick Victorian home. (Berger had arranged his figures so that they looked out all the windows, until local residents complained.) By now the museum has spilled over into a refurbished garage and two other buildings. I was shown around Vent Haven one afternoon by Don Millure, who is a trustee, and his wife, Dorothy, who is the curator. Nine McElroy figures are on view, including one, named Kenny Talk, who can smoke a cigarette and blow the smoke out his ears. Harry ("the Great") Lester's Frank Byron, Jr., is there, and Valentine Vox's Cecil Wigglenose. There are replicas of Edgar Bergen's Charlie McCarthy and Paul Winchell's Jerry Mahoney. Farfel, the dog figure that Jimmy Nelson used in his famous series of Nestlé's Quik commercials, peers down from a shelf with heavy-lidded eyes; actually, this Farfel is the original Farfel's stunt dog, the one that would get shot out of a cannon and do other dangerous deeds. In one room, on row after row of folding chairs, an audience of perhaps a hundred figures sits with open eyes and vacant smiles. The effect of this grouping is overpowering.

There is something surreal and ghastly about a ventriloquist's dummy. In its life on stage it serves as a source of entertainment, but in its private life, we all know, it is an all-too-willing slave of dark forces, a characteristic displayed in movies like *Dead of Night* (1945) and *Magic* (1978) and in television programs like *The Twilight Zone* and *Night Gallery*. At the Vent Haven Museum there are some six hundred of these beings, clustered together in mobs of sixty to a hundred or more. Some of them have human hair or teeth. Virtually all their masters are long since dead, yet here sit the dummies, intact and immortal, though torn forever from their original voices. One dummy on display was found amid the rubble of a German house destroyed during the Second World War. Four others, from the turn of the century, were washed ashore after a shipwreck, the only survivors. On the walls, arrangements of photographs show the great ventriloquists of yore getting older and frailer; the agelessness of their partners seems to mock them. A ventriloquist who came to the museum with me pointed out a certain figure and said, "The first time I saw him sitting there, I nearly broke down. He belonged to a friend who had just died in an accident." A visitor to Vent Haven whose thoughts do not somehow touch on death is probably not human.

The association of ventriloquism and death has a historical basis. Some figures at Vent Haven go back 175 years, and the books there about ventriloquism go back even further, but the origins of the art itself lie deep in antiquity. Necromancers, who advertised themselves as the living vessels through which the spirits of the dead could speak, apparently were able to transmit aperçus from the underworld without labial agency. There is archaeological evidence for this from Egypt and Palestine, and literary evidence from all over. (The biblical story of the Witch of Endor, in Samuel, is thought to involve a ventriloquist.) Up through the Middle Ages ventriloquism remained a tool of those with avowed ties to the supernatural. Elizabeth Barton, the so-called Holy Maid of Kent, professed such ties when, in a trance-like state and with no visible movement of her mouth, she suggested to Henry VIII that divorcing Catherine of Aragon would not be such a great idea. The suggestion was itself not such a great idea. Barton was hanged at Tyburn in 1534.

Not long afterward, of course, came that famous sea change in Western civilization when the realm of the spirit was invaded by scientists and entertainers. No one really knows who first established himself as a professional vent, but by the nineteenth century ventriloquists were fairly common. They usually didn't use dummies, however, but entertained their audiences through exhibitions of the distant voice. This minimalist approach, whose effect can be dazzling, is one that some of the best modern ventriloquists take during portions of their acts. The use of mechanical figures was popularized in the late nineteenth-century English music hall, where ventriloquists generally used not one figure but a whole family of them, often affixed to a bench: a blackamoor, a sailor, an old woman, a clown — the combinations varied. The first man to become well known for using a single figure seated on his knee was Fred Russell, an English ventriloquist who flourished in the 1890s. A triumphal tour of the United States at the turn of the century by Arthur Prince, another English vent who used a single figure, made ventriloquism wildly popular in this country and shaped its contours for years to come. Harry Lester, who saw Prince perform, made his debut in 1902 and became the premier American vent of the vaudeville era. It was the Great Lester who taught Edgar Bergen (a $300 check from Bergen to Lester for lessons is on display at Vent Haven), and it was Bergen who led the way out of vaudeville and into broadcasting, inspiring Winchell, Nelson, and others. The example of Winchell and Nelson in turn helped draw in the generation that is now achieving prominence, on television (especially cable) and in clubs — people like Lucas, Dunham, Jay Johnson, Alan Semok, and Willie Tyler.

Why, I asked Dorothy Millure, do so many ventriloquists' figures tend to look alike? She said, "That's a legacy from the old days, too. There used to be a stock character in vaudeville, the wisecracking Irish kid, and ventriloquists, who worked vaudeville, realized early on that this was the perfect sort of foil. That's why your typical figure has a black Irish look and a name like Danny O'Day or Jerry Mahoney or Charlie McCarthy. Of course, that's all changing. You've seen the dealers' room. In thirty years the people in the museum" — I raised an eyebrow — "will be a lot more diverse." One major trend is toward the use of soft figures made of cloth or foam. The classic hard figure with a headstick will always be popular, but soft figures are within the financial reach of more people, especially young people, than hard figures are. They are also simpler to manipulate: you can use your hand directly to move the mouth and face rather than having to negotiate a headstick. The advent of soft puppets is often cited as among the contributing factors in ventriloquism's resurgence.

I had dinner after my tour of the Vent Haven Museum with a Chicago-based vent and figure maker named John Arvites. Like a number of prominent vents, Arvites acquired his skills not through schooling but at the side of a "great man" (in this case, Frank Marshall). One of Arvites's primary figures now is a hard dummy of a wizened black man named Little Charlie, who is supposed to be more than a hundred years old. Arvites is white. I brought up the subject of the ventriloquist's dummy's evolving form, and he said, "Some things have changed. Vents now tend to use mixed styles of puppets. There are also some things that don't change. People will listen to a figure more readily and attentively than they will listen to a real person. The psychology is strange. You can say things through a puppet that the audience would never accept from you yourself. Whether I'm in a blues club on the South Side of Chicago with old Charlie, at a corporate banquet with Fred the Guy, or in a school with Terry — in any of these situations any of my characters can say things that the audience will think are delightfully funny, but if I had said them myself I'd get killed for it.

"Your characters are tools, instruments with which you communicate. The key is to create an illusion of life. It's a game of make-believe in which you act as if the puppet actually had a life of his own. You'll find yourself being surprised by things that the figure says — things you would never think of saying yourself."

Ventriloquists don't really regard their figures as beings with an independent existence, but watch a vent put his dummy down and you'll see that he never just throws him on a table or into a trunk. He almost always sets him down gently, in a chair. I heard a story from Jimmy Nelson. He was taping a show for television, and the script involved Nelson, the dummy Danny O'Day, the dummy Farfel, and Nelson's wife, Betty. Everything went fine until it was Danny O'Day's turn to speak. "I remember looking at him," Nelson said, "and thinking, 'C'mon, the lines aren't that hard.' But he didn't say a word. My wife had to kick me."

—◆◇◆—

When I said earlier that ventriloquism was a career path I had forsworn, I wasn't quite telling the truth. Anytime I have a puppet on my hand and a child on my knee, something compels me to become a not-so-great Lester. Anyone can be a successful vent when the audience consists of a single three-year-old and when the words to be said are easy ones, like "Hey, guys!" or "Are you a duck?" But when the situation calls for you to say something like "Shut up and listen, you bloody fool," even a three-year-old will catch your lips moving. This is because *p, b,* and *f,* together with *m,* are the Scylla, Scylla, Scylla, and Charybdis of ventriloquism, and doom most passing lips.

I sat down for a cup of coffee one afternoon with Bob Isaacson, a ventriloquist who lives in Oak Park, Illinois, and asked how a ventriloquist makes the *b* sound. Isaacson said, "Well, some books will tell you to substitute a *d* sound, but I found when I was just learning that that doesn't quite make it. 'How adout a dottle of deer?' Or some will say to use a *v* sound. 'How avout a vottle of veer?' When I first started, I remember thinking, 'This isn't very good. This isn't very good at all.' I started thinking in my mind a combination of *d* and *v.* An exaggerated version would be, 'How advout a dvottle of dveer?' And I just kept trying it over and over again, trying to slide the sound out. And eventually it came to sound like 'How about a bottle of beer?' 'How about some beer and some baked beans?' See, that wasn't bad. Of course, you get the *b* down and you still have the other hard ones to master. The most common substitution for *p* is a *t.* 'Do you want to buy a tickle for a nickel?' 'Teter

Titer ticked a teck of tickled tetters.' Sometimes a *th* works better. 'How about a thickle?' 'How about a pickle?' 'A thickle.' 'A pickle.' That's not too bad. Again, it depends on how you slide that sound out. It's almost a slurring kind of thing. Some people use an *f*. 'A fickle.' 'A pickle.' I'm kind of blowing the sound past my lips."

Isaacson went through the other tough sounds. The extraordinary thing about our conversation was that during most of it Isaacson never moved his mouth. From three feet away I was aware of the expulsion of air and of tense undulations in the muscles of Isaacson's neck, but that was all. I went back to my room and began to practice what I had just learned, bearing in mind the exhortatory mantra in Paul Winchell's *Ventriloquism for Fun and Profit*: "Don't rush. Don't get impatient. Don't get discouraged. Don't ever give up." I gave it a good fifteen minutes. Then I got impatient and discouraged and gave up. I went out and dought a dottle of deer.

People like me, who aren't in the business, tend to think that making the hard sounds without "flapping" ought to be just about enough to qualify you as a real ventriloquist, but in fact it only makes you eligible. Vents do kid around about the oral tricks they resort to — I was introduced to the ventriloquist Colonel Bill Boley by a vent who called him Dill Doley — but they don't pretend that letter substitutions, however skillfully voiced, are more than a small part of the illusion. One night I saw a boy with a gorilla dummy on his arm go up to one of the bigger names in ventriloquism. I heard the gorilla say, "Hi, friend, my name is Big Boy." And the older vent said, "That's pretty good, son. But how's your distant voice? How's your muffled voice?"

I sat in on a good many seminars at the convention — how to survive a kid's show, constructing a foam-head puppet, putting mouths on things — and one of the most memorable, conducted by a vent named Nacho Estrada, was devoted to the distant voice. You are likely never to encounter Estrada unless

you are in high school or grade school and live in the Southwest.
He goes from one school district to another, cutting deals with
superintendents here and there and offering funny but serious
programs about all the familiar touchy subjects. He limbers up
his larynx while driving to shows by singing the famous refrain
from "Witch Doctor": "Ooh, Eee, Ooh-ah-ah, Ting-tang, Walla-
walla Bing-bang." Estrada is esteemed among his peers for his
mastery of the distant voice.

He explained in his seminar that a voice from a distance was
different from the regular "vent voice," that the individual words
had to be drawn out longer — "Heeeey, Joeeey" — and that the
voice had to lose much of its body and texture, becoming forced
and tiny. "You have to talk from your stomach," he said. "Or
like the way you would talk just after somebody punched you
in the stomach." (The word *ventriloquism* comes from the Latin
for "talking from the stomach.") But then Estrada went on to
say that voice technique was never enough by itself, that voice
can't give itself a false source. He had performed a routine at
the seminar in which his dummy was in a trunk whose lid he
kept raising and lowering, and the dummy's voice, which seemed
to be coming from the trunk, was modulated accordingly in
loudness, pitch, and sonority. Or so it seemed to me. Estrada
said, "There's no such thing as throwing your voice. Your voice
has to come out of your mouth, because that's where it comes
out of. Fortunately for us, the ear isn't a very reliable organ. It
doesn't always know where a sound is coming from. It will associate itself with any visual cue that happens to be around.
If a sound suddenly sounds muffled when I'm closing the trunk,
people think it's happening because I'm closing the trunk. If
I didn't have a trunk, they'd probably think I was just lowering
my voice."

Any vent will tell you that manipulation and the figure's personal character are as important as the vent's voice in the success
of an act. I had several conversations at the convention with
Alan Semok, who is a figure maker and actor and a very suc-

cessful vent. Semok's first dummy was given to him when he was a child to help him overcome his shyness, which is a story that not a few vents tell. (Another story vents sometimes tell is that they were given their first dummy for companionship during a serious childhood illness.) Semok had this to say about manipulation: "When you look at a lot of beginner vents, you notice that their voice is fine but their figures are dead. Basically it's just the mouth that's moving. And the vent winds up having this magician problem, where the audience spends all its time looking at *him*, wondering if he's going to slip up. The audience is supposed to be more interested in the dummy. Edgar Bergen had terrible lip control — actually, it was good at first but deteriorated after he worked in radio — and nobody cared, because Charlie McCarthy was just so real."

I have seen Semok's point borne out twice. The first time was when I was a child and saw Paul Winchell and Jerry Mahoney do a show that was a spoof of a Charlie Chaplin short and had no spoken words. It must have been entrancing, because the memory is still vivid and I was only four or five. The second time was at the convention, when Jeff Dunham performed one night with a dummy of sour mien made by the figure makers Bill Nelson and Chuck Jackson. Dunham's manipulation, perfected on the daunting machine that is a McElroy, can be exquisite, and the dummy he was manipulating that night was unusually expressive to begin with. For fifteen minutes the dummy, which looked vaguely like François Mitterrand, drew laughter with little more than an occasional grunt, a raised eyebrow, a disgusted turn of the head. "Something must be wrong," Dunham said later, "when you can get by in an act without your figure having to talk." He was being too modest.

—◆◇◆—

Contests are held throughout the International Ventriloquist ConVENTion, for juniors and seniors, and prizes are awarded for distant voice, manipulation, and originality. One night I saw a boy of ten standing in the hallway with a typical Irish-kid type of dummy on his arm and his mother bending over him. He was in tears because he had arrived late and missed his chance to compete in the juniors. On the next night the convention officials interrupted the senior competition and gave the boy his turn.

He came out onstage dressed in immaculate white and with the confident presence that very young people sometimes have, not being aware yet of all the good reasons for falling to pieces. His dummy, it seemed, had been lonely of late, didn't have any friends. "You always have a friend," the boy told him. "No, I don't have any friends," the dummy insisted. "Yes, you do," the boy said. I didn't have to wait long to find out where this routine was leading. A few moments later I heard the dummy say, "Jesus? I don't know any Jesus." And off it went. When the boy finished, he slid from his stool and sang, in a high, clear voice, without accompaniment, a hymn. About half the people in the audience rolled their eyes and clapped dutifully, and about half gave the boy an authentic ovation.

You don't notice them at first, because the more pungent aspects of the art, such as dummies and disembodied voices, tend to make a more forceful initial impression at the convention, but gospel vents are a growing force in ventriloquism. Clinton Detweiler estimates that 50 to 70 percent of the people taking courses from the Maher Ventriloquist Studios intend to use their talents for church work. In the dealers' room, a good number of stalls offered a selection of materials of a plainly Christian provenance, such as a *Treasury of Clean Teenage Jokes* and *Gospel Ad-Vent-ures*. I was struck at the convention by how inoffensive the humor was in general, and eventually learned that this was the result of a tacit compromise between the gospel vents and the others. Some friction had been growing between the two groups as the presence of gospel vents at the convention became increasingly pronounced. Tensions were eased when the gospel vents began to do less "witnessing" onstage and to use the convention mostly to exhibit their secular material. (They can strut their gospel stuff at the annual convention of the Fellowship of Christian Puppeteers.) The other vents, in turn, tried to bear in mind that they weren't in Las Vegas.

I had dinner with Dale and Liz VonSeggen, who direct the Puppet Ministry of the Denver First Church of the Nazarene, and after Liz had blessed our food, she said, "You don't get much of an inkling at first that people like us are here. Several years ago there was an attempt to run two separate programs, one for club performers and one for Christian performers. A decision was reached after that to combine our efforts. A lot of the evangelicals now tend to pull back and cross over to main-stream vent routines. But we come because this is the greatest gathering of ventriloquists in the world, and it's the only place you can go where everyone understands your artistic needs."

Dale VonSeggen said, "You probably think puppet ministry is a little strange, but puppetry has been associated with religion for a long, long time. The word *marionette* means 'little Mary' and comes from the Middle Ages, when Christmas plays would be performed with puppets. Then puppetry was thrown out of the church, and it stayed out for a long time." It was accepted back by the Protestant churches in the nineteenth century and received a great impetus in the 1970s, with the popularity of *Sesame Street.* "We figured," Dale said, "that if you could use figures to teach the ABCs, you could use them to teach John 14:6." An enterprise called Puppet Productions, in San Diego, sent teams around the country, mostly to fundamentalist churches, to set up puppet ministries for children. Demand grew rapidly, and Puppet Productions eventually branched into programs aimed at combating drug and alcohol abuse.

The ability of a puppet or a dummy to command attention, compel confidence, and force a message through is difficult to counter. Puppeteers and ventriloquists are now routinely used to elicit testimony from children who have been beaten or sexually abused and who won't talk to an adult. But church work is by far the largest nontheatrical outlet for ventriloquism. Liz Von-

Seggen received her first dummy, a Danny O'Day replica from a mail-order catalogue, in 1964. The VonSeggens now rule a small empire. When I spoke to them, they were about to embark on an eight-city cross-country tour with their evangelical troupe, called Victory in Puppetry. They conduct a week-long Children's Ministries University every summer, attended by two hundred people.

Gospel ventriloquism has made at least one small inroad into an older faith. Jonathan Geffner, who was my pick to win the seniors competition (he came in second), started out as, in his words, "the Jewish equivalent, I guess, of the gospel vents." Geffner, an intense young man, has a master's degree in piano from the Manhattan School of Music. He turned to ventriloquism in part because he was having trouble making a living in the concert hall. He began using ventriloquism in classes he teaches in Hebrew school, and his Jewish theme programs soon became popular in temples, community centers, and schools throughout the New York area. He now performs a wider range of material.

I asked Geffner what he especially liked about being a ventriloquist. He thought for a minute and then said something I had been told in various ways by other vents: "Well, there's the whole element of not having to rely on another human being."

—◆◇◆—

"I don't know — maybe it's the element of miracles," Ronn Lucas said when I asked him why there are so many evangelical ventriloquists. "Maybe they read about Moses talking to the burning bush and it gives them ideas. This is one of those unanswerable questions. Why are so many famous ventriloquists left-handed? Why do a disproportionate number seem to come from Texas? I don't know the answer to those questions either."

Lucas was relaxing in his suite, dressed in a jumpsuit. I asked Lucas if ventriloquists have a code they live by, and he laughed and said, "You mean a Ventriloquitic Oath?" He thought for a while. "There are some things that generally aren't done," he said. "The vent's voice has to be his own, and it has to be live, or at least appear to be. And the figure on his knee is traditionally something he manipulates, not a real person. But there are always legitimate exceptions, and there's room to stretch. There's a lot that can be done with electronics, for example, to change the character of your voice or enable you to manipulate a figure from afar. It's inevitable that ventriloquism will branch out into holograms and liquid crystal displays. But what will always remain the same is the schizophrenic aspect of ventriloquism, the tension between illusion and reality, that both attracts and repels."

Lucas took Buffalo Billy down off a chair.

"I hate having to get up," Billy said. "Reality is getting me down. Reality is so phony."

"But Billy," Lucas said, "you're not real."

"Can I take that as a compliment?"

III

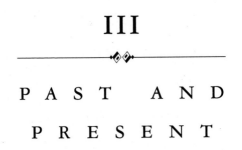

PAST AND PRESENT

On Rewind?

—◆◇◆—

F O R E W A R N I N G S   O F

T H E   F U T U R E

I POURED MYSELF a glass of iced coffee one morning recently, and as I was taking it over to where I wanted to sit, I stumbled. A little of the coffee spilled out of the glass and onto the table. I looked at the spill, and then looked again: it was exactly the shape of Nantucket.

My thoughts flew at once to Maria Rubio, of Lake Arthur, New Mexico. In the fall of 1977 Rubio was cooking a tortilla in a skillet when what she believed to be the face of Jesus suddenly appeared on it. Her home was soon besieged by thousands of devout pilgrims. A few years later, in Hidalgo, Texas, a similar image appeared on a tortilla being prepared by Paula Rivera, and the Rivera home, too, drew throngs of the devout.

I had intended at first not to say anything publicly about my own kitchen epiphany, fearing an onslaught of J. Crew models and Episcopalians. ("No doubt about it, John. That's Great Point." "And look! The Starkweather place.") But a few days afterward came a phone call and with it an invitation to visit Nantucket. Now I had to confront a troubling question. Had that spilled arc of iced coffee been merely a coincidence? Or was it — dare I say — a portent?

At some deep, limbic level of sentience, most of us, I suspect, have not quite given up on the idea that portents may and do occur. I have never had much truck with oracle bones or necromancy or the entrails of sheep, but I do remember as a youngster sometimes aiming a baseball at a distant lamppost and saying to myself that hitting it would be a sign that . . . well, that some desirable thing of the moment would come to pass. And if the ball missed on that first attempt, the portent threshold in my mind would quickly be altered: the ball might need to hit on only one throw out of three (okay, five). One day, while reading A. J. Cronin's *The Green Years,* I discovered that the book's narrator, Robie Shannon, sought an answer to an important question about the future by throwing pebbles at — yes! a lamppost. At the very least, this was a vindication. For all I know, it may even have been a portent.

The problem with portents, of course, is that only in hindsight can they be shown to have predictive power. A truly valuable portent would reveal itself as such unequivocally and in the present — would take us for a moment to a high place affording a confident view of the unfolding landscape of contingency that stretches to the horizons of time. In reality we know what the high place was only by looking back from the low ground of the future, and we tend to forget all the times when the vista proved to be a mirage. Mark Twain believed that his birth in a Halley's Comet year presaged his death the next time Halley's Comet came around, seventy-five years later. The only reason anyone remembers this fact is that we now know Twain was right. Similarly, the embroiderers of the Bayeux Tapestry knew by the time they set to work that the comet suggestively filling the sky in advance of the Battle of Hastings (Halley's again) really had been a portent of William the Conqueror's invasion. In contrast, I am at a loss to identify even a few initial portents to be worked into a Bayeux Tapestry of my own life. I know that I was born in the midst of a violent hurricane, which my family still refers to as "the night of the big wind." Is that how the embroiderers should begin? Somehow, I hope not.

Portents are fickle. They may deliver moments of revelation that defy understanding and save the day, but just as often, whether because believed and acted upon or because disbelieved and not acted upon, they can become bound up with terrible events. A few days before the Ides of March, Julius Caesar was told by an inspector of entrails that no heart could be found in a bull that Caesar had ordered to be sacrificed — a bad sign. Caesar made his fateful trip to the Senate anyway. Croesus, king of the Lydians, tried to do everything by the book. As Herodotus tells the story, Croesus wanted to know his prospects in an impending war against the Persians. Determined to find out which of various oracles around the Mediterranean was reliable, he sent out messengers to them all, asking them to describe what he would be doing on a particular day. The oracle at Delphi got it right: Croesus on that day would make a stew of tortoise and lamb. The oracle then delivered this prediction, which Croesus accepted unreflectively: "If Croesus makes war against the Persians, he shall bring to the ground a great empire." Croesus did, and the empire he destroyed was his own.

Nowadays, of course, we have tools other than portents with which to grope toward the future, chief among them the science of statistical forecasting. This science got its start in the seventeenth century (one of its pioneers, and the first person to compile actuarial tables for human lifespans, was Sir Edmund Halley), and it pervades Western thinking about the consequences of everything from personal relationships to medical procedures to government policies. It is portentousness bureaucratized. Is it also an advance? One can certainly say that statistical forecasting has reduced the possibility of wild error even as it has made more remote the likelihood of breathtaking definitiveness. A few years ago a professor at Princeton announced in the British journal *Nature* that statistical manipulations alone could show with a 95 percent level of confidence that *Homo sapiens* would last at least another 5,100 years but not more than another 7.8 million years. The mathematics here is apparently unassailable, and I have made a note on my calendar. But does this even compare to Babe Ruth at the plate pointing his bat to right field?

If the idea of portents has lost some of its ancient luster, a companion notion may be on the verge of winning new credence. Even if it is not possible ever to gain a true glimpse of the future, one could experience something like the same sensation if time began to run backward. I am aware, of course, that Stephen Hawking, in *A Brief History of Time,* has argued that time cannot really go backward (although his book does prove that time can be made to stand absolutely still). It may very well be that scientific experiments, perhaps using Albania and Paraguay as controls, would show that time in some technical sense is marching onward as robustly as ever. Yet I can hardly be alone in feeling that at some point during the past decade or so, the tide of human affairs commenced a slow and uneven recession.

I am no student of cosmology, but I have long been of the view that before our species ends its run — sometime, that is to say, in the next 5,100 to 7.8 million years — we will all be told, as if by an angry parent, "Now, I want everything put back the way it was. Neatly!" Signs that this process, sure to be an unruly one, may already be under way are gathering rapidly. The most obvious indication involves the entire Eurasian landmass, where the dissolution of the Communist empire has suddenly made maps printed in 1911 once more in demand, along with members of various indigenous royal families. But there are many other signs of a gradual return to the way things used to be. For example, the Church of England, which broke with the papacy in 1534 over the issue of Henry VIII's divorce, has entered a period of what may be terminal chaos; growing numbers of its adherents are returning to the Church of Rome. The people of the Netherlands, who spent much of the past millennium turning sodden marsh into dry land, are now for environmental reasons taking vast tracts of dry land and turning them back into marsh and open water. The Japanese, who during an invasion of Korea in 1597 collected the noses of twenty thousand enemy soldiers and civilians and then took the noses to Japan and put them in a shrine, have now given all twenty thousand noses back to the Koreans.

The idea that civilization has embarked on a process of rewinding must for now remain a matter of speculation, but I hope to have something further to report on the matter very shortly. I have just two more throws to go.

The Way We Were

—◆◆—

A CRO-MAGNON

LIFESTYLE

THERE IS a famous saying of Bacon's to the effect that modern times are really the oldest ones (the world, after all, is not getting any younger), and that what we think of as antiquity, "by a computation backwards from ourselves," was actually a time of youth. This is an attractive and nicely counterintuitive notion, and one that is nearly impossible to keep in your head as you go about daily life. People just don't tend to think this way. And yet we all feel powerfully the loss of youth, especially if ours has been misspent; we have similar feelings about the lost youth of our race, about a world that was brasher and less proud and perhaps more suited to our natures. The myth of the noble savage may have been given a name by Rousseau, but it is probably one that even noble savages entertained.

What is surprising, though, is not that we harbor an affectionate attitude toward times gone by — many things, including beer, literature, and New York City, did use to be better — but that we so often move beyond passive nostalgia and attempt to bring back the past. I would not go so far as to say that civilization's every step forward compels a compensatory step in retreat, but it does seem to me that as society ratchets onward, there is always a bit of slippage in the gears. The last few millennia offer several thousand examples, but let me present some from my own lifetime.

The La-Z-Boy reclining rocker, a state-of-the-art platform for the human frame in sentient repose, was introduced in 1961, well in time for the first Super Bowl; it was countered by that strange pretzel-shaped chair with no backrest which is supposed to be the ideal seating arrangement for creatures who were once arboreal. In the late 1960s the design of running shoes became a focus of Space Age ingenuity; the Stone Age response, in the early 1970s, was the Earth Shoe, a sloped-backward affair designed to induce the natural gait of Brazilian aborigines. In 1982 the first Jarvik-7 artificial heart was installed in a human subject; around the same time doctors began taking a second look at the medicinal properties of leeches. More recently, in the dawning age of the computerized, or "smart," house, there have been reports of people choosing to live underground or in caves.

This sort of thing — this resuscitation of the old and even of the primitive — is happening all around us, and once one becomes aware of the pattern, its new manifestations seem eerily predictable.

That is why students of the phenomenon sat up and took notice when the trade journal *Frozen Foods Age* reported that sales of frozen convenience dinners, which had increased by 33 percent in the course of a single recent year, had achieved a historic high. Within months of this news the inevitable counterpunch was delivered, in the form of an article in *The New England Journal of Medicine*, "Paleolithic Nutrition: A Consideration of Its Nature and Current Implications." The article, by the physicians S. Boyd Eaton and Melvin Konner, bluntly asserted the superiority of Cro-Magnon Man's diet. The article has since been expanded into a book, one that offers not only a "program of diet and exercise" but also a complete "design for living."

The Paleolithic Prescription, by Eaton, Konner, and Marjorie Shostak, an anthropologist, opens on a needlessly defensive note:

"To some people, this book will be worth a lot of laughs." Oh, there are sure to be those who will have their fun ("Pass the mammoth, please"), but in the main the argument of the book strikes me as unassailable. *Homo sapiens,* the authors say, evolved in the context of a certain environment and way of life. For the most part, the conditions to which man was ideally suited no longer obtain, and yet man himself is little changed in any fundamental genetic way. We are still turning out the basic Cro-Magnon type of fellow, except that now he is working at a desk job, is afflicted by high levels of stress, is eating foods he wasn't meant to, and, not coincidentally, is looking forward to a date with high blood pressure, diabetes, cancer, and heart disease.

In contrast, the cave person, according to *The Paleolithic Prescription,* was lean, tall, strong, and aerobically fit. He did not smoke. If he drank, it was haphazardly. If he liked meat, it was meat that was low in fat, because wild animals have a lot less fat than domesticated animals do. And he consumed a good deal of roughage, apparently about three pounds of raw vegetable matter a day. Cave persons also got lots of exercise. And they were not really the benighted captives of traditional sex roles we make them out to be. "If human societies were ranked along a continuum according to the status of women," the authors write, communities of cave persons "would be positioned near the end closest to full equality." Chronic degenerative disease, by the way, was almost unknown.

It sounds almost too good to be true, and in one or two particulars maybe it is. Some scientists argue that cave persons consumed more sugar, especially in the form of honey, than other scientists have cared to acknowledge. Rhodesian Man, a Paleolithic citizen whose remains were uncovered in Zambia, has been described by one analyst as a "dentist's delight." As for alcohol, a controversial new theory holds that not only did cave people have a taste for it, but they made the leap to agriculture precisely in order to be assured of reliable supplies of grain for beer. An archaeologist friend of mine has also pointed out that

whereas cave persons may have been aerobically fit, we all might
be if we shared our dwellings with eighteen-foot-tall cave bears.
We might suffer a bit from hypertension, too.

Still, *The Paleolithic Prescription* makes good general sense,
and I am giving serious thought to it. I am troubled, however,
by the authors' tolerance of halfway measures, by their insufficient zeal. They note, for example, that cave persons were ardent
insectivores, and yet nowhere on any of their suggested menu
plans do insects, which are rich sources of protein, appear; rather,
we are urged toward the usual vapid substitutes, such as chicken
breasts (skinned) and cottage cheese. And though we are informed that your typical cave person, for all his clean living and
egalitarianism, lived to only about thirty years of age, the matter
is simply dropped and the provocative implication left unpursued.

Can I be alone in wondering whether a human lifespan limited to three decades or so isn't what God really intended, and
isn't such a bad idea regardless? Most of life's minor irritations
are, to be sure, caused by people under thirty, but most of the
real damage to the world has been done by people who are
older. If life ended at thirty, the occasional Alexander the Great
would still wreak havoc from time to time, but the First World
War would never have happened, and probably neither would
the Second. We would still have most of Mozart but a lot less
of Friml. If life ended at thirty, there would be no more Dr.
Ruths, nor more aging rock stars, no more graduation speakers
of the most compulsory and tiresome kind, and no more nostalgia booms that couldn't be dismissively put down. The Social
Security Trust Fund would turn into pure plunder and could be
used to pay off the federal deficit. And no one, at long last,
would be eligible to run for president of the United States.

I would be surprised if such a regime, provided that it was
adequately grandfathered, did not find wide acceptance.

The Tithe

—◆◇◆—

DOING THE RIGHT
THING BY POSTERITY

THE CARTOONISTS Dik Browne and Mort Walker once wrote a book called *The Land of Lost Things,* in which a little boy, having become separated from his parents, finds himself in the mythical place where all lost things go. The bewildered boy is surrounded by car keys and mittens and teddy bears, by baseball gloves and twinless socks. Eventually, of course, he makes his way out.

The land of lost things, settled entirely by immigrants, has its share of emigrants, too — of things that return, often after long absences, to the world they came from — and the emigrants are almost always welcomed back with warmth and delight. I was reminded of Walker and Browne's book by news of the chance discovery in London, during construction of an office complex on the Thames, of the foundations of the Rose Theatre, where Shakespeare's first plays were performed. The event aroused enormous public support for the preservation of the site.

Several years ago a stir was created by the discovery in Greece of the remains of Philip of Macedon, a man who paid tuition bills to Aristotle and whose tomb no one had ever hoped to find. Earlier, Leonardo's notebooks and the Dead Sea Scrolls won broad public interest and acclaim when brought to light after many centuries. As a teenager, I started saving newspaper accounts of discoveries like this — "33 Bach Organ Preludes Are Discovered at Yale"; "A Scholar's Find: Shakespearean Lyric"; "Soviet Writer Says He Has Found Bodies of Czar and Family" — but the seas of time washed the yore upon the now so regularly that finally, with Canute-like resignation, I gave up. Yet each new report in the press ("Chesterton Aphorisms Found in 2d Writers Book") provides a curious sense of reassurance. Even when the discoveries contribute nothing of importance, really, to our stock of knowledge or beauty, they at least suggest that though the past may one day lock us up, it won't necessarily throw away the key.

The uncovering of the Rose Theatre raises a disturbing question, however. Is the modern world doing its duty by future generations and losing enough splendid things for posterity to find? There is reason to believe, I fear, that the supply of future *objets trouvés* is being diminished in two ways. On the one hand, what we wish to destroy is today destroyed with an absoluteness of which the ancients were rarely capable and to which they rarely aspired. For example, no equivalent of a Wailing Wall remains from the original Madison Square Garden. On the other hand, a growing preservationist impulse, combined with the advent of mass production, makes it harder for many things to become lost in the first place. Will a copy of *The Godfather* ever not exist? There is a remote possibility, I suppose, that statistically the matter is a wash — that because we are making so many more things than we used to, the same number of significant artifacts might be left behind as have always been. But I don't think so. During the past two and a half decades, for example, only a couple of things have gone missing that our grandchildren would be excited to find: eighteen and a half minutes of a tape recording made in 1972, to name one, and perhaps Jimmy Hoffa. Compare this dismal legacy with that of a typical year in antiquity — 612 B.C., say, when the entire city of Nineveh was consigned to oblivion in a single day.

The time has come, I think, for concerted action. I would propose the levying of a national tithe, whereby a certain percentage of what is new and of social or cultural importance — 10 percent seems about right — is simply squirreled away in some odd place. Under such a regime (to illustrate), Philip Roth would not actually have published his tenth novel, *The Professor of Desire*, but instead would have delivered the manuscript to a government functionary, who in turn would have deposited the work in a trunk (say) in the attic of a country house in Scotland (say); the functionary would then have been sworn to secrecy, or shot. A similar procedure could be followed with paintings, television shows, movies, presidential documents — anything, really. The bodies of some of our significant dead (perhaps every tenth person whose passing is noted in *Time*'s "Milestones" column) should be treated in the same way. The English have been doing this willy-nilly with their monarchs from the start. King Edward the Martyr (975–979) didn't turn up until 1931, when he was found by a gardener in Dorset; he was stored until recently in a cutlery box in Woking, England, pending the outcome of litigation. The whereabouts of William the Conqueror (1066–1087) are unknown to this day, save for a single thigh bone, discovered in France in 1987.

One last detail: much of what turns up unexpectedly raises piquant problems of identity. Those bones of Philip's — are they really his? That Shakespearean lyric — truly Shakespeare's? This vexing quality adds mystery and spice and ought to be encouraged. I see no reason, for example, why the title page of the hidden *Professor of Desire* might not conveniently have become detached, or why some future pope should not be buried, in full regalia, in Muncie. We may not be around for the headlines, but we will have had our fun.

Nostalgia for the Dark Ages

—◆◈—

DUSTING OFF THE

OLD CORVÉE

ST. MARY'S COUNTY, Maryland, is a triangular piece of turf defined by the confluence of the Chesapeake Bay and the Potomac River. Settled by highborn English papists in 1634, it is the oldest jurisdiction in the state. On a recent visit to St. Mary's, I noticed a banner slung above Route 5, scored here and there by half-moon incisions to accommodate gusts of wind. It advertised a jousting tournament to be held at Horse Range Farm, in the town of Mechanicsville.

Jousting is not unusual in Maryland. Thanks to the efforts of Henry Fowler, the master of Horse Range Farm, who for many years represented his county in the house of delegates, the joust has since 1962 been Maryland's official state sport, although combatants eager to be "well seene at armes" now spear dangling rings rather than "tourney one against one, or two against two," as William Caxton would have had them do in the fifteenth century. Even so, hundreds of Marylanders have gamely taken up the lance.

They are not alone, at least not in spirit, for the rehabilitation of the medieval has been under way in the United States for some time. Long derided as "Dark," and consigned by Peter Mark Roget in his thesaurus to a forlorn suborder of the category "Ignorance," the Middle Ages today are downright fashionable. Symbolic of this change in fortune was the success of Umberto Eco's medieval thriller, *The Name of the Rose*. Despite its untranslated Latin apothegms and daunting disquisitions on scholastic philosophy, the novel sold three hundred thousand hardback copies (at $15.95 apiece) and graced the *New York Times*'s bestseller list for almost twelve months.

In academe, the number of courses on medieval subjects has been on the rise for years, as has the number of students taking them. According to a survey by the medievalists Christopher Kleinhenz and Frank Gentry, during the decade ending in 1980 thirty-seven new scholarly journals specializing in the Middle Ages commenced publication. Since 1970, attendance at the annual conference of the Medieval Institute at Western Michigan University, in Kalamazoo, swelled from eight hundred to almost two thousand, making it the largest medieval *congressus* in the world.

Meanwhile, clubs and confraternities dedicated to medieval pursuits have proliferated across the continent: the Harlotry Players (Ann Arbor), the Society for Creative Anachronism (Berkeley), the Poculi Ludique Societas (Toronto), the International Early Dance and Music Institute (Amherst), and scores of others. Groups like these, some of them more serious than others, sponsor tournaments and revels, masques and mystery plays, seminars and summer schools, all in an attempt, as the Society for Creative Anachronism would have it, "to create a total medieval environment."

This sort of thing has also been creeping out of the university towns and into affluent suburbs. On the verdant fringes of the nation's 323 Standard Metropolitan Statistical Areas, hardly a weekend now passes without jugglers, buffoons, mummers, and minstrels strutting about in some public park. As enthusiasts in period costume dance a saltarello to the strains of cithara and bombulum, onlookers may sample black pudding and turnip jam and fend off the chill with noggins of hippocras and perry.

Are the Middle Ages worth the fuss? In Kingsley Amis's novel *Lucky Jim,* the protagonist, a lecturer in medieval history, delivered one opinion, and at first glance his argument seems compelling: "Those who [profess] themselves unable to believe in the reality of human progress ought to cheer themselves up . . . by a short study of the Middle Ages. The hydrogen bomb, the South African Government, Chiang Kai-shek, Senator McCarthy himself, would then seem a light price to pay for no longer being in the Middle Ages. Had people ever been as nasty, as self-indulgent, as dull, as miserable, as cocksure, as bad at art, as dismally ludicrous, or as wrong" as they had been during the Middle Ages? Possibly not, a fair-minded person is bound to admit.

Indeed, in certain respects the medieval period seems to have been a calamity, the ill effects of which have persisted to this day. Writing in the newsletter *Humanities* in 1982, the historian Norman Cantor argued that sizable chunks of our medieval legacy will have to be jettisoned "if the world is to become peaceful and secure or even to endure." He cited as examples "the dead hand of bureaucratic oppression," a rigid social hierarchy, "violence against peaceful minorities," and "imperialist greed" spurred by religious intolerance. But Cantor discerned gold amid the dross. He noted that the jury system, common law, parliamentary institutions, the hospital, the university, and the "high market value for the skills of artists and scholars" are all medieval hand-me-downs. To this list one might add scores of other worthwhile innovations that have not survived, among them the ducking stool, the king's touch for scrofula, and the practice of fining college professors who lecture past the bell, skip portions of the syllabus, or fail to attract at least five students to each class.

My own view is that in its haste to leave the Middle Ages behind, the West discarded much that was of value, junking countless customs, institutions, and serviceable quirks of sentiment that might easily have been adapted (with happy results) to the altered conditions of subsequent centuries. Fortunately, it is not too late to set things aright. Given the popular esteem for the Middle Ages, the time may be ripe for a revival of useful practices sadly fallen into desuetude — a bit of backpedaling, as it were, in the interest of progress.

For example, there has been much talk in recent years about requiring the young to perform some sort of "national service." Surely we might consider instead dusting off the old corvée, which entitled a lord of the manor to an unspecified number of days of what we now would call "community service" from every tenant in his seigneury. With nary a day's warning, Bodo could be called on by his master to plant a hedge or plow a new assart, and Bodo's wife might be summoned to the "big house" to help with the cooking and sewing. An updated, democratized corvée, run by local governments or perhaps the Salvation Army, has its possibilities. The conscripts might even receive modest compensation. As the historian Marc Bloch noted in his book *French Rural History,* "Although compulsory, work done as a corvée was not necessarily unrewarded; the lord was sometimes obliged to provide refreshments."

In the realm of jurisprudence, trial by ordeal would certainly help clear the dockets. "Tell me, pray," demanded Saint Bernard in his *De Consideratione,* "what is the good of litigating from morning till evening, or of listening to litigants?" Eight centuries later, we still have no acceptable answer. While trial by ordeal is plainly unsuitable in criminal proceedings (where right, often as not, has already succumbed to might), it could prompt speedier resolution of corporate lawsuits and deter nuisance libel actions. Imagine the time, money, and aggravation that would have been saved if General William Westmoreland and Mike Wallace, or Lillian Hellman and Mary McCarthy, instead of hunkering down to protracted litigation, had each been required to grasp a bar of red-hot iron, with the judge ruling in favor of the party whose hand was not burned.

As for foreign relations, we would all breathe easier for a new Truce of God. The Truce of God initially forbade warfare only on Sundays, but the prohibition was later broadened by the Church to include the six weeks of Lent as well as every Thursday, Friday, and Saturday (the theory being that good Christians needed three full days to prepare for Sunday worship). Applying this rule to the Jewish Saturday and the Muslim Friday, and throwing in Ramadan and all of the festivals and High Holy Days, along with the various Hindu *utsavas* and the many Buddhist anniversaries and *uposatha* celebrations, we would be left with only an occasional Monday on which to come to blows.

Regarding the conduct of our daily affairs, the monastic *Regula Sancti Benedicti,* composed by Saint Benedict during the sixth century A.D., still has much sound advice to offer. "If you have a dispute with someone, make peace with him before the sun goes down." "Do not love immoderate or boisterous laughter." "As often as boys and the young . . . are guilty of misdeeds, they should be subjected to severe fasts or checked with sharp strokes."

Which of us, moreover, has never been thwarted, frustrated, or misled by the curt receptionist, the vapid ticket clerk, the officious lobby guard, the obstinate bureaucrat, and other inhabitants of postindustrial America's waxing Cerberus sector? Here again we would do well to heed the sage Saint Benedict. He advised his brethren, "At the door of the monastery, place a sensible old man who knows how to take a message and deliver a reply. . . . As soon as anyone knocks, or a poor man calls out, he replies 'Thanks be to God' or 'Your blessing, please'; then, with all the gentleness that comes from the fear of God, he provides a prompt answer with the warmth of love."

The Longest Day

—◆◆—

CIRCLING

STONEHENGE

THE SUMMER SOLSTICE always falls on the twenty-first or twenty-second of June, and on that morning an observer standing at the center of Stonehenge and looking toward the northeast will see the sun rise over the summit of the so-called Heel Stone, which stands a short distance beyond the megalith's perimeter. Actually, the sun appears slightly to the left of the Heel Stone's blunted apex, but the sight, I have been told, is impressive all the same. Not many people in recent years have been able to see it, however. Stonehenge has, it seems, become a gathering place on the summer solstice for many of those in Britain who have adopted a lifestyle at variance with mainstream insular tendencies. Some of these people are young, trailer-based itinerants whose purpose in life appears to be (in the words of press accounts) to "alarm local authorities." Others are white-clad adherents of the ancient Druid cult, which seems rapidly to be displacing the Church of England as an outlet for popular piety in Britain. Come late June, mobs of such enthusiasts have been converging on the chalk downs of Wiltshire for the solstitial sunrise. But for reasons of security Stonehenge on that day has been surrounded with coils of barbed wire and an ample detachment of policemen.

I spent a morning at Stonehenge not long ago, on a day when very few people were there, and grew immediately fond of the place and its irrational appeal. For one thing, it fails to disappoint one physically. I have heard the Pyramids and Mount Rushmore belittled by people who have seen them, but I have never heard an ill word about Stonehenge, which is smaller and far less handsome. The reason, I think, has to do with its setting. Stonehenge can be seen across the flat open fields of Salisbury Plain from a mile or two away, and one's eyes naturally gravitate to the only big object in the landscape for which chlorophyll is not responsible. The structure is also remarkably old — some five thousand years old. Archaeologists did not know this until the mid-1960s, when radiocarbon dating and its astute employment by the British archaeologist Colin Renfrew forced them to abandon all the previous theories about how architectural advances had been exported to the barbaric northern lands from the Mediterranean and the Middle East. (Stonehenge, it turned out, predates the elegant Greek citadel at Mycenae.) No one knows quite how the ring was constructed or what it was used for. It rises from a plain that is pocked with hundreds of burial mounds and scarred by the soft depressions of neolithic tracks and ditches — obviously quite a place in its day, though now given over to farmland and, a bit to the north, a military base. Walking over the landscape nearby provokes all kinds of reflections. Almost every rise and depression in the fields was deliberately constructed, for reasons that are often not fully understood, thousands of years ago. Someone who died when Ozymandias reigned could be responsible for your spraining an ankle.

Stonehenge was old, and perhaps already a curiosity, when the Romans, and after them the Angles, Saxons, and Jutes, came to Britain. One can only speculate about what any of these people made of the place, since their opinions on the subject have not come down to us. But they certainly noticed it. The Romans left coins and pottery at the site, and the Anglo-Saxons gave Stonehenge its name. It is probably safe to assume that they all read meaning into Stonehenge from the comfort of their own world-view. This seems to be what everyone whose thoughts we know about has done. The Normans — one of whom, around A.D. 1130, composed the earliest written reference to Stonehenge that has survived — wove Arthurian legends around the ring to glorify the British past. In the eighteenth century, some writers enthralled by the pastoral ideal saw Stonehenge as the Jerusalem of Druidic ritual and depicted the Druids, who are known to have practiced human sacrifice, in terms that today might apply to Unitarian members of the Green Party. (As it happens, no evidence links the Druids and Stonehenge at all.) In our time, thanks largely to the efforts of an IBM computer and the astronomer Gerald Hawkins, whose book *Stonehenge Decoded* was a bestseller in the United States in 1965, Stonehenge has come to be regarded by many not merely as a remarkable example of primitive engineering but as a mini Mount Palomar, an astronomical observatory of surprising sophistication, capable of predicting eclipses of the sun and the moon. That the phrase "ancient computer" now elicits instant comprehension when associated in the press with any enigmatic lithic structure is mostly Hawkins's doing, and I pretty much assumed until very recently that Hawkins's word on the matter, however refined by other scholars, was the last one.

Apparently, however, this is not the case. I had a chance to speak with Colin Renfrew, who teaches at Cambridge University, and he explained that few of his British colleagues today subscribe to the Stonehenge-as-observatory theory and that, furthermore, "I'm not sure that many of us ever did, really." It seems that the weight of British archaeological opinion, which can be ponderous indeed, has fallen in behind a contrary view. Yes, the British scholars say, the alignment of some of Stonehenge's stones, such as those that point approximately to the places on the horizon where the sun will rise on the longest day of the year and set on the shortest one, was undoubtedly deliberate. But most of the other proposed alignments have no significance whatsoever and can be explained as the inevitable product of coincidence in a structure that once contained more than 150 stones in more or less circular patterns and that stands beneath a sky whose own patterns are cyclic. (One archaeologist has noted that even the Oval Office, if it had a few more windows, could be shown to be a primitive observatory.)

I frankly resisted this humbler view of Stonehenge, perhaps because I had derived a successful high school career in science in no small part from the work of Professor Hawkins, but the evidence in favor of it seems overwhelming. For one thing, the apparent coherence of the structure is an illusion; it was built in fits and starts, with new features canceling out old ones, over a period of about fifteen hundred years. And it is not obvious how Stonehenge is supposed to work; proponents of the Stonehenge-as-observatory school have put forward half a dozen different theories. What this suggests, as the archaeologist Christopher Chippindale recently observed, is that "if you toy with Stonehenge for long enough, you are sure to come up with something astronomical it can be made to do."

It may be that Stonehenge will forever stand as one of those few ancient monuments about which one can say little more beyond mere description than that a couple hundred generations of people have felt the urge, for one reason or another, to get close to it. And it may be, too, that ignorance about the place underlies its enduring appeal. Unlike the Maya temples, unlike the Circus Maximus, Stonehenge has nothing about it that prompts unpleasant associations, and perhaps for this reason it seems permanently fresh and available for use. Stonehenge has been replicated on the banks of the Columbia River in Washington State as a war memorial; in Missouri, at the state university in Rolla, as an observatory; and in Blackstock, Canada, as a tribute to the crushed cars from which the replica there has been fashioned. It appears in advertisements for cameras, computers, and cigarettes and has lent its name to housing developments and hotels. Stonehenge figures therapeutically in the novel *A Mag-*

got, by John Fowles: "He pointed to a great stone that lay imbedded flat beside others that still stood and told her to lie upon it, for such was the superstition, or so he said, that a woman taken there might help a man regain his vigours." And, of course, there are the Druids and the itinerants, not to mention a breed of crank antiquarians, hardy perennials on the British scene, with their exotic opinions, their ample supplies of stationery, and their propinquity to a free press. So many tourists visit Stonehenge every year and unwittingly degrade the site that some thought has been given by the directors of the English Heritage Commission, which looks after the monument, to erecting a full-size replica nearby. The replica would perhaps be made of Styrofoam or Fiberglas; it has been referred to in the tabloids as Foamhenge.

I expect that Foamhenge, being just the sort of project against which cooler heads can be counted on to prevail, will not actually be built, and that is a pity. A synthetic Stonehenge might last forever and would be plagued by few of the maintenance problems that have beset the original monument. More important, it would be certain to baffle future generations. Scholars five thousand years from now would have to ask themselves not only "What was it for?" but also "Why are there two?" And the one who guessed right would probably never be taken seriously.

The Future of Pennies

—◆◇—

O U R   F I R S T   L I N E

O F   D E F E N S E

A POLL conducted a few years ago by the newspaper *USA Today* revealed that 37 percent of Americans surveyed would be in favor of eliminating the penny from the nation's lineup of currency — a percentage, apparently, that has been steadily on the rise. The case for eliminating pennies as a pocket-filling irrelevance is even being pressed by a lobbying group in Washington called the Coin Coalition.

The suggestion that the United States get rid of pennies is, like many proposals that smack of cool-headed, cold-blooded pragmatism, one that should be implemented on another planet. It is the kind of apparently sensible yet hugely disruptive reform that a wise society will treat with the same disdain that America has already shown for the metric system and phonetic spelling.

Should we stop making cents? The penny we now have was issued in 1909 to celebrate the centennial of our sixteenth president's birth, and its name and ancestry go back to the eighth century. From the start the penny's biggest foe has been inflation, which has for centuries threatened to render the coin valueless. And yet monarchs and prime ministers have deemed this insufficient cause to rid themselves of it, preferring to let the penny

be and to invent higher denominations of currency — as when
Edward II established the groat. Indeed, by its continued existence the penny has served notice that the value of money cannot
be infinitely debased, that the monetary systems of the English-
speaking world have an anchor, albeit a shifting one. As long as
the penny exists, there will be things you can buy with one or
two or three or four of them. Get rid of it and nothing will cost
less than a nickel.

That is the economic defense of the penny. Pennies also serve
important social functions. They inform millions of children
who may have been exposed to nothing but textbooks that there
once was a man named Lincoln who occupied a position of
some importance. They are responsible for initiating millions of
conversations in stores every day between people who otherwise
would complete their transactions in anomic silence. From time
to time these transactions are punctuated by mild bleats of satisfaction — "Wait, I have a penny!" Such moments, occurring
all across the nation and around the clock, contribute modestly
but directly to social comity.

Pennies, moreover, are so deeply embedded in our culture that
extracting them would leave small emptinesses in the very substance of life. Pennies help to mark the stages of life. They are
the first allowance we receive. Later we put them on railroad
tracks, and then in loafers, and later still in fuse boxes. Inevitably the day comes when a penny falls from the hand and one
decides not to pick it up. In the mature adult this prompts a
fleeting sense of contentment, for he has acknowledged the fact
of his own security. We wish on pennies at fountains and wells,
knowing that dimes and nickels won't work. In a pocketful of
change, pennies serve as an essential garnish, relieving an otherwise drab monochrome like radishes in a salad. And in our
language they are called upon liberally when precepts of formidable consequence must be conveyed. "Look after the pennies
and the pounds will look after themselves." "A penny saved is

a penny earned." Thanks to exhortations like these, it may very well be that if all the pennies hoarded in bowls and jars were taken into account, the often maligned U.S. savings rate would approach that of Japan.

The elimination of the penny might afford some slight physical convenience, but the total social cost exceeds what a liberal democracy ought to countenance. It would be nothing less, one might say, than penny wise and pound foolish.

Survivors

———◆◇◆———

STILL IN

SHADOWY EVIDENCE

A FEW MONTHS AGO, finding myself in the vicinity, I called at Poplar Forest, the house Thomas Jefferson built near Lynchburg, Virginia, as a refuge from the crush of visitors at Monticello. The house, a brick octagon, was in private hands until a decade ago, when it was acquired by a group intending to restore it. Poplar Forest has neither the grandeur of the University of Virginia nor the quirky intelligence of Monticello. The house is elegant but simple, and one can imagine oneself actually living in it.

For the time being, one can also appreciate the building in a state of minimalist purity. As part of the restoration process the interior walls have been stripped of plaster and trim, and the entire house is now a bare brick shell. Looking closely at the walls, though, one can see signs of how the house has been altered since Jefferson's day. Certain features in the brickwork indicate that many of the windows were once higher. A fireplace set in a wall now looks small, but the faint outline around it of a much larger mantelpiece shows that the design once made it grander. Throughout the house, patterns of small gouges in the mortar hold the secret of lost details of the original interior woodwork. In an odd way, the house Thomas Jefferson knew still exists inside this shell. I was pleased to learn that all those faint but unmistakable indications of a building's former state are known to architectural historians as "ghosts."

The tides of time and history can be as capricious in what they preserve as in what they carry off. At the end of the Second World War, the tides mysteriously swept from its repository in Berlin the hoard of treasure unearthed by Heinrich Schliemann at the site of ancient Troy, in 1873. A few years ago they suddenly tossed the treasure back into public view. (The Russians had it all along.) One can only be grateful for such acts of restoration, and for other instances of unbidden bounty — the revelation of a Tut's tomb, a Tara brooch, a Boswell's diary. But the acts of preservation I appreciate most are less stunning and complete, more delicately indirect, and have above all a certain aloofness: the things being preserved come a certain distance forward and no further. One may think of them, like the masonry lineaments at Poplar Forest, as ghosts.

A possibly fanciful but widely discussed recent example was provided by Michael Crichton in his book *Jurassic Park,* in which he held out the possibility that if, many millions of years ago, an insect bit a dinosaur and was then trapped and preserved in amber, the DNA of that dinosaur might yet be extracted from the blood in the insect's thorax. Scientists have not gotten as far as the blood in an insect's thorax, but they have amplified and sequenced DNA from an extinct species of weevil entombed in amber some 120 million years ago, and have done the same for bees and termites entombed in amber 25 to 40 million years ago.

Most of the dwellings occupied by people in prehistoric and imperial Roman times have long since disappeared from the European countryside. But remnants of structures survive beneath the surface — walls and foundations, filled-in pits and ditches — and affect the retention of moisture, which in turn may retard or enhance the rate of growth of grain directly above relative to that of the grain all around. On some mornings, when the sun is strong and low, the taller stalks cast shadows on the shorter. If the field is viewed from above, the outlines of buildings and enclosures stand out clearly, as if in an architectural drawing. The apparitions vanish as the sun climbs toward midday and then reappear before sunset.

In cities and towns throughout Europe, buildings down the centuries have been erected abutting major structures that themselves were slowly eaten away. A precisely shaped vacancy preserves the soul of the departed: the oblong Piazza Navona, in Rome, once a stadium; the elliptical Piazza del Mercato, in Lucca, once an amphitheater. In their way these public spaces evoke the private cavities in the hardened volcanic ash at Pompeii, which, injected with plaster, reveal ghosts of their own, the recumbent forms of the victims of Vesuvius.

Ghosts come in many mediums. In the museum at the Los Alamos National Laboratory, a test tube holds sand from a beach on an island in the Pacific that no longer exists, having been destroyed during the testing of a thermonuclear device. Of the handful of signatures that there are grounds for believing may authentically be Shakespeare's, one can be recognized as such only because it bled through the page to the underside, from recto to verso. The mirror-image version — the signature as seen from behind — is the only version now legible.

By their very nature the visual arts provide an abundant supply of ghosts. In his book *The Lost Museum,* the historian Robert Adams devotes himself to "the work of art that is no longer around to speak even stutteringly for itself, but which speaks nonetheless through a secondary veil or mirror." He notes, to give one example, that while only the Wailing Wall survived the razing of the temple in Jerusalem by the Romans in A.D. 70, we do actually know something about what the temple's furnishings looked like, because images of plundered objects were sculpted in bas-relief on the Arch of Titus, in Rome. Another example from Adams: Sir Anthony Van Dyck's famous triple portrait of Britain's King Charles I — left profile, full face, and right profile, all on one canvas. The painting may be admirable in its own right, but it was originally intended to serve merely as "notes" for the sculptor Bernini, who was working in Italy on a bust of the king. It is now our only link to that bust, which was destroyed in a fire in 1698.

In a category of their own are paintings that survive only inside other paintings. We no longer have the Franz Hals picture titled *Woman with a Pipe,* for example, but it appears hanging on a wall in the background of two different paintings by Jan Steen. The genre of painting known as gallery painting is a rich secondary source. Prominent collectors in the seventeenth and eighteenth centuries would commission artists to paint pictures of their galleries, whose walls were closely hung with works of art. Not surprisingly, some of the paintings in those galleries — real works for which there is documentary evidence — were somehow later destroyed or can no longer be found. The only record of what they looked like is their depiction in gallery paintings. Willem van Haecht's *The Picture Gallery of Cornelis van der Geest* ("Geest," appropriately enough, means "ghost") contains several pictures of lost artworks, including *Marriage Bath,* by Jan van Eyck. There is something especially haunting about the situation of these paintings within paintings. Visitors from a three-dimensional world, they are now stranded for eternity in two dimensions, accessible to the touch and yet impossibly remote.

One does not need to look to the world of architecture or archaeology or fine art in order to find ghosts. This, to my mind, is one reason why they have such resonance. They can be vestiges of a distant past, but they are also a presence in daily life. They are pervasive, of course, in our speech. In metaphor and simile, and in the very building up of words, we preserve prior meanings and carry forward a record of conditions and concepts that may no longer be current. "Mad as a hatter." "Hold your horses." "Rake over the coals." The science of etymology amounts, in a way, to tracing the genealogy of ghosts.

Ghosts crop up elsewhere. Think of unfaded rectangles on the wall where pictures used to be, or the small depressions in the carpet that the removal of furniture leaves behind. Driving down a country road that has been straightened once or twice, I notice how the curves of the old route occasionally braid in and out of the new one. When I open a book I haven't read in many years, I'm sometimes surprised, even chagrined, by ghosts in the form of my marginal notations, evidence of reactions to the text ("!!???") that must once have been pregnant and powerful but that now elude full apprehension. Often when riffling through old photocopies, I come upon pages in which a person's fingertips or the ball of a hand can be seen along an edge, surely belonging to someone I know.

I worry that ghosts are becoming too common, losing some of their magic, as methods of secondhand preservation proliferate. In 1961 Goya's celebrated portrait of the Duke of Wellington was stolen from the National Gallery in London. The movie *Dr. No,* which appeared a year later, shows James Bond doing a subtle double take when he sees the painting on an easel in Dr. No's undersea lair. Of course, the only reason the picture could be shown is that copies of it existed, by the thousands. Photographs and computers have enhanced the prospects for the survival of almost anything. Broadcasting sends messages into infinity.

Even so, as I was reminded one day recently, the role of serendipity remains. I was walking through a park, absorbed in thought and oblivious of the world, when I heard a faint *click* to my left, followed by nervously polite laughter to my right. I looked up to see that I had strayed at exactly the wrong moment between a prosperous Asian man with a camera and his carefully posed family. At least part of me is now playing the role of *Woman with a Pipe* in an album far away. It's good to know, in case something happens to the original.

All the Pope's Men

PUTTING AQUINAS
TOGETHER AGAIN

JUNE 1979

THE VIA APPIA rolls across the Pontine marshes and hugs
the Italian coast between Naples and Rome, but the Via Latina,
several miles inland, was always the preferred route of Thomas
Aquinas, preacher general at the University of Naples, regent
master in theology at the University of Paris, Angelic Doctor,
Dominican priest, philosopher, saint.

He was born in 1225 at the castle of Roccasecca, which guards
the Via Latina near Aquino. While traveling along the road
forty-nine years later, he struck his head against an overhanging
branch and suffered the subdural hematoma to which, latter-day
physicians surmise, he presently succumbed. The Church mourned
the loss of its philosopher, struck down in his prime. Yet when
death took Thomas on that March morning in 1274, he was in
fact broken, physically and mentally. He had written nothing in
three months, and when pressed by Reginald of Piperno, his

scribe and friend, explained darkly that "after what I have seen," everything he had published "seemed as straw."

Thomas entered religious life at the age of five, groomed by his parents to become (like his uncle) abbot of the Benedictine abbey at Monte Cassino, a position of considerable power. Thomas shunned the prospect, foiling his parents' plans by joining the Dominicans, an impoverished, mobile, and studious order of priests founded by Dominic de Guzman in 1216. The rule of the order was strict. Thomas was obliged to walk wherever he went, be it to Rome or Paris, Lyons or Cologne. This may account for his complexion, which contemporaries compared to "ripe wheat." He was a hulking, gentle, tongue-tied man, nicknamed the "Dumb Ox" by his Dominican brothers. Albert the Great, Thomas's teacher, was of another opinion. Someday, he predicted, his pupil's bellowing would "resound throughout the earth."

Saint Thomas today enjoys exalted status as the Roman Catholic Church's foremost theologian and philosopher. (His is the only proper name to be found in the Code of Canon Law.) In times of intellectual crisis, the Church has often rested its weight on Thomistic philosophy, as it did during the Counter Reformation and, three centuries later, during the Modernist controversy. In the *Summa Theologiae* and the *Summa Contra Gentiles,* Thomas himself took on the doctrinal threat from Greek science and philosophy (lately reintroduced into the West by the Arabs) and in the process systematized Christian theology in Aristotelian fashion. The first of these works was written for "beginners," the second for "unbelievers," which perhaps helps to account for the attractiveness of Saint Thomas to thinkers in the centuries since.

—◆◆◆—

There is a congenial stretch of the Via Latina thirteen miles southeast of Rome that Thomas Aquinas knew especially well, where the road slices through catacombs and into the Alban

Hills. The water was good, and nearby were family friends, at Molara Castle. Thomas stopped at the castle one day with Reginald of Piperno, who was dying of tertian fever. The doctors had given up hope. That night, Thomas placed some relics of Saint Agnes on his friend's chest, and Reginald recovered at once. According to an eyewitness, the household celebrated with "special solemnity and a good dinner."

The incident accounts for one of a paltry three miracles Thomas is reputed to have performed during his lifetime. (He later cured a woman "afflicted with a flow of blood," and several days before his death changed some sardines, which he disliked, into herrings.) The "devil's advocate," whose official task it was to oppose Thomas's canonization as a saint, deemed these insufficient signs of sanctity. Pope John XXII disagreed, generously allowing, in 1321, that Thomas had performed as many miracles as he had resolved philosophical questions. Since the *Summa Theologiae* alone contains 512 questions, 2,669 articles, and some 10,000 objections with replies, Thomas's elevation to sainthood was approved forthwith.

Barring a miracle we don't know about, Thomas would not have been familiar with the present friars' house in the village of Grottaferrata, several hundred yards from Molara Castle and the Via Latina. There, at the command of the pope and under the banner of an organization known as the Leonine Commission, Dominican priests are toiling to bring forth, in the original medieval Latin, the first critical edition of Thomas's three great theological syntheses, nine disputations, twenty-seven commentaries, five polemics, six treatises, five expert opinions, sixteen letters, and seven sermons. The project was begun under Pope Leo XIII, one hundred years ago; another hundred years may see it finished.

The Leonine editors take a special interest in Aquinas because as Dominican priests they are sworn to reverence his person and defend his writings. With their colleagues in Rome, Washington, Louvain, and Ottawa, the scholars at Grottaferrata have spent every day for thirty years poring over thousands of medieval manuscripts from places such as Erfurt, Parma, Prague, and Zwettl. They have been given, by successive popes, the freedom of the Vatican Library — the rarest of privileges — and have been known to take Aquinas's seven-hundred-year-old handwritten drafts home on the bus — rather like getting leave to borrow a Van Dyck or two from the Hermitage.

Unfortunately, since few of these original drafts, or autographs, have survived, reconstructing a single book as Thomas presumably wrote it can take up to fifteen years. Often the editors are reduced to working from sloppy, error-filled copies or even more corrupt copies of copies, generations removed from the philosopher, the theory being that since everything in the Middle Ages had to be copied by hand from something else, *some* link back to Aquinas must exist *somewhere*. Elaborate family trees of each manuscript are constructed, revised, and discarded. "At times," says Grottaferrata's prior, Father Louis Bataillon, "one feels like Inspector Maigret."

Every friar has a specialty. Father René Gauthier, the librarian, is casually known to his brothers at Grottaferrata as Aristotle. He works from early morning until late at night, and his sharply chiseled features discourage idle conversation. He can tell at a glance whether Aquinas was using the twelfth-century *Anonyma* translation of Aristotle's Greek *Metaphysics* or Michael Scot's thirteenth-century version.

Other Dominicans relish the minutiae of ink, and can judge in seconds whether a manuscript was written with sour gall or Aleppo gall, with green or blue vitriol, with the lees of wine, black amber, sugar, or fish glue. Father Jordan Peters, a Dutch Dominican, is one of those who can discern the difference. "French and Italian inks," he explains one day, "are blacker than English and German, and Spanish is the darkest of all." A handy maxim.

Father Peters works out of a cluttered, parchment-laden office at the University of Saint Thomas Aquinas (or Angelicum) in Rome, a prestigious Dominican school whose alumni include

Pope John Paul II. His feel for a text is subtle and exact. He eyes the format of the page, deftly probes the shapes of the letters, then glances at the method of abbreviation. The verdict: "English, late thirteenth century. When Englishmen put strokes above letters to make abbreviations, the strokes were usually connected with the final flourish of the last letter they had written." He points to the manuscript. "See, like this:

A Frenchman would have lifted his pen."

The twenty-two friars who make up the commission receive no pay for their work: all have taken a vow of perpetual poverty, along with vows of chastity and obedience. The Dominican order provides every priory with a small stipend for each priest, and the money is held in common. "If I want a box of cigars," explains Father Peter Gils, a Leonine editor who works out of Louvain, Belgium, "I go to the *syndicus,* the priest who handles our cash. There is rarely any problem." The friars live a monastic life of prayer, contemplation, and arduous scholarship little different from the life Aquinas lived. They lack only the luxury of living to see their work completed.

It is not as if they have never known, or wanted, another life. Father Bataillon, sixty-five, was trained as a lawyer. He helped manage a Breton fishing port before becoming a Dominican. Father Bertrand Guyot, fifty-nine, who lives with Bataillon at Grottaferrata, was trained originally as a mathematician — "*Mathématiques pures, pures, pures,*" he insists. Father Joseph Cos, fifty-seven, came to the job after seventeen years as a missionary teaching Latin and Greek in the Congo. While he was on leave in Belgium, rebel tribesmen slaughtered his companions and colleagues. He volunteered for the commission. Father Hyacinthe Dondaine, eighty-six, a mathematician and friend of the theologian Jacques Maritain, didn't even join the Dominican order until he was thirty-five. And Father William Wallace, sixty, the current (and first American) president of the Leonine Commission, was originally an engineer; he supervised the aerial mine-laying effort that cut off Japan from Korea and Manchuria during the Second World War.

So far the Leonine editors have published thirty-two elegant, red-and-black, leather-bound folio volumes of the works of Saint Thomas — some fourteen thousand pages in all. In addition to possessing a meticulously reconstructed text, each volume is densely glossed with Latin footnotes. Until recently, the lengthy explanatory prefaces were also written in Latin — in finely wrought Latin, if Father Gauthier's is any indication.

There are about thirty volumes to go. But the commission has been plagued by bad luck from the start. The combination of wars, meddlesome pontiffs, and lack of money is a historic combination for disaster. At times the work of the commission has slowed to a trickle; occasionally it has stopped altogether. Today, the Leonine editors may be facing the greatest crisis yet, as the thirteenth century squares off for a final bout with the twentieth.

Simply put, they are running out of talent, and out of time. Recruits to the Dominican order are down sharply, part of a general trend throughout the Roman Catholic Church. Moreover, Latin, once the Church's lingua franca, has been dropped from every seminary in every nation on the globe, a consequence of Vatican II reforms. Yet a knowledge of Latin — specifically, of medieval Latin, medieval handwriting, and medieval abbreviation — is the *sine qua non* of membership on the Leonine Commission. "We would train our successors," Peter Gils says, "if there were anyone to train."

Morale on the commission somehow remains high, with a sense of humor as ironclad a prerequisite as fluency in Latin. Often the latter gives rise to the former. (At the commission's Washington branch, precious manuscripts are stored in a stout safe. The combination: *Verte ad sinistram quater usque ad sexaginta septem, ad dextram . . .*) But the handwriting is on the wall. Of the twenty-two Leonine editors, fifteen are over fifty-

five years of age, nine are over sixty, and two — Father Hyacinthe Dondaine and his brother, Antoine — are into their eighties. There is no one under forty.

In a report to the master general of the Dominican order in
Rome, Father Wallace noted that while most of the remaining
volumes of the Leonine edition have been either started or as-
signed, "there is doubt that the work can be maintained." Father
Wallace's report, composed in Latin down to the financial statement of *acceptis et expensis*, is not a happy document.

Sales of Leonine volumes, mostly to university libraries, are
steady but slow. Last year the commission sold two sets of Aquinas's *Summa Contra Gentiles*, bringing the total number sold
since 1965 to almost one hundred. From the commission's point
of view, the *Contra Gentiles* has been a successful volume, but
revenues (each book costs $50) hardly cover the $1 million the
editors have spent in the past fifteen years. Hiring laymen to help
with the work is out of the question. (Several laymen — like the
medievalist James T. Reilly and the paleographers Carlo Grassi
and Bernardo Bazán — donate their time to the commission.)

Father Gils, in Louvain, believes that "fifteen well-trained scholars working every day for fifty years might just be able to finish
the job." But in cold, clinical terms, the Leonine Commission
may not have fifty years or even thirty, and in twenty years it
may not have fifteen men.

—◆◆—

I first learned of the Leonine Commission from Father Avery
Dulles, a Jesuit theologian. I laughed when he told me that the
commission had already spent two of Aquinas's lifetimes trying
to edit what the saint had managed to write in twenty-two years.
"It was the common view," wrote Bartholomew of Capua, "that
[Thomas] had wasted scarcely a moment of his time." What
would Bartholomew have thought of the Leonine Commission?

I drove out to Catholic University shortly afterward for lunch
with Father William Wallace, who in 1976 succeeded the late

(and by all accounts remarkable) Father Pierre de Contenson as president, or *praeses,* of the commission. Father Wallace is an active, youthful-looking, gray-haired scholar, a specialist in sixteenth-century science and the author of, among other books, *The Scientific Methodology of Theodoric of Freiburg* and *Galileo's Early Notebooks.* He is also an immensely popular teacher, as comfortable with colleagues at the Institute for Advanced Study in Princeton as he is teaching philosophy of science to a class of one hundred nurses. It is not hard to understand why Charles Sweeney, on the eve of his mission over Nagasaki, sought out Father Wallace for a late-night conversation on the ethics of the atom bomb. (Both men were serving with the 313th Bomb Wing.)

Father Wallace is somehow worldly, urbane, a man of affairs, even when resplendent, with dangling black rosary, in the long white robes of his order. He displays a quiet, energetic confidence that would have taken him to the top in any profession, a characteristic shared with every member of the Leonine Commission.

He lives with eighty other Dominicans at the Dominican House of Studies, a vaguely Flemish Gothic building inflicted on the Catholic University campus earlier this century. When blueprints of the house were sent to Rome for approval, Church authorities promptly wired back: *"Sintnē angeli?"* — "Are they angels?" The architects had apparently left out the bathrooms. Most amenities are available now, including a secular food service that provides the Dominicans with meals. (The shortage of personnel makes an outside service a necessity.)

After noon prayers, the Dominican friars gather for lunch in a long, spare refectory, its windows opening onto a columned cloister.

"What most people want to know," Father Wallace says, "is why the work is taking us so long. That's also what the pope wanted to know. Our first three volumes were published soon after Pope Leo established the commission in 1879. That wasn't fast enough. Leo was a Thomist, one of the leaders of the neo-

Thomist revival of the late nineteenth century. What he really wanted was a *new* edition of the complete works, not a good edition. He wanted it yesterday, for the seminaries. And he wanted the *Summa Theologiae* first. The Leonine editors were under a gun."

When Leo's intentions became clear, the Dominicans severed financial ties with the pope. That left them in semiautonomous penury. Since then, with the exception of some modest crumbs from the pope's table — $10,000 from Paul VI in 1966, for example — the Dominicans have financed the venture by themselves. Thanks to the order's vow of poverty, the labor is free, but printing costs are high, in part because French linotype operators in Limoges, setting pages in Latin, can't tell when they've made a mistake. There is never enough money. Hence the limp in the commission's gait.

"Then there is the matter of standards," Father Wallace says. "We had to invent our own. Nothing like the Leonine edition has ever been done before. How can you tell what Thomas's text really was? We have only a handful of his handwritten drafts but an embarrassment of corrupt copies, thousands of them, spanning two centuries. How do you grope your way back? And where are all the manuscripts in the first place? Library science and ancient documents do not get along. I was in the Biblioteca Nacional in Madrid in 1967 when they found Leonardo's 'lost' notebooks. They weren't lost. They were just on the wrong shelf for hundreds of years."

Father William Conlan, a wry, bespectacled Dominican, is sharing our table. He joined the Leonine Commission ten years ago and now spends his time collating: comparing manuscripts, plotting every difference and discrepancy, every changed abbreviation, every jot and tittle of variance, trying to determine the provenance of each, to deduce the father from its spawn. Where was the manuscript transcribed? Was it copied from an original draft by Aquinas? Dictated? Copied from another copy?

The work spins off on tangents. "We have to know how the

publishing industry worked in Paris," Father Conlan explains. "After all, that was how Saint Thomas's books got around. We have to know what copies of what books he was using. We're working here on his commentary on Aristotle's *Metaphysics.* Thomas used three different translations of the book at different times. Maybe four. It's a nightmare."

Sorting things out is complicated by the fact that few medieval scribes, scholars, or painters ever signed their work. Of the four score surviving manuscripts of the *Metaphysics,* for example, only one is signed (by John of Frankenstein). The Leonine editors regard scribe John's signature as a breach of taste. They themselves cherish virtual anonymity. The names of a Leonine volume's editors are mentioned only once, if at all, in the preface, in six-point type.

—◆◆—

From the perspective of today it is hard to gauge the immensity of the Leonine Commission's task. But consider a worst-case scenario beginning, say, in 1256. Young Thomas is teaching at the University of Paris. He rises before dawn every morning to prepare the lectures he will turn into books. He is living at the Convent of Saint Jacques on the Left Bank, where Latin is so prevalent that despite ten years in Paris, he has never learned French.

It is a crowded university, overrunning the Latin Quarter with its ninety buildings and its great array of Irrefragable and Invincible Doctors. The noise from the narrow street filters in through the windows where Thomas is lecturing on the *Sentences* of Peter Lombard. In 1256, the university is seething with anti-Dominican sentiment, and the archers of King Louis IX — Saint Louis — stand guard atop the roof of Saint Jacques to quell disturbances.

Has Thomas written out his remarks on Lombard? Probably. If he has, they are scribbled in a fast, sprawling hand that resembles pigeon tracks in sand. (He was never taught calligraphy.) Even in the thirteenth century it was known as the *littera illegibilis,* and Thomas's closest associates, including trusty Reginald of Piperno, had nearly as much trouble reading it as modern scholars do.

After class, Thomas amends and revises his lecture, then gives it to one of his secretaries to make a fair copy. If the Leonine editors are lucky, Aquinas's handwritten draft will survive for seven hundred years, enabling them to go right to the Ox's mouth to establish the restored text.

Usually the editors are not lucky. In the case of the commentary on Lombard, scarcely one fourth exists in autograph. So they must work instead from the secretary's copy, or from copies of *his* copy. Thomas's secretaries are diligent men, but after all, they are only men. They strain to read his writing. If the penmanship is especially atrocious, Thomas may fall back on reading his writing aloud. The solution is fraught with its own problems: the secretary misses words continually, his ear plays tricks on him, he misunderstands the meaning of a sentence, he skips a sentence.

When the dictation or copying is over, Thomas examines the transcript. Of course, he is a busy man. He is hard at work on *Being and Essence* and a half-dozen other works. It is Lent and he must prepare for the fortnightly *quodlibetal* ("what-you-will") discussions, off-the-cuff debates at which he is the target. The atmosphere at the university is tense, and Thomas is a nervous man. Perhaps he doesn't give the editing the time it deserves. His citations are not quite exact. Even when they are, the text he is using may be faulty.

Assume that Thomas, despite the inevitable errors, approves a version of his lecture to be "published." A clean copy, or *exemplar,* is made and deposited with the university *stationarii* — "vulgarly called booksellers," according to one early document. The *exemplar* is divided into *peciae,* loose sections of eight pages each. The *peciae* are then rented out individually to students for copying. In the days before printing, there was no other way for textbooks to be circulated.

Now the trouble begins.

Let us say that Odo, a young Flemish student, wants to make a copy of Aquinas's commentaries on Lombard. By 1286, nineteen of Thomas's works were available in the university bookstore. The commentaries on Lombard, in 215 *peciae,* rented for ten solidi.

Odo goes to the stationer and rents, for a week, the first *pecia.* Since his family has made a killing in textiles and his father is grudgingly generous, Odo needn't do the transcribing himself. Instead, he engages one of the poorer students to do it for him, a common practice.

The student is from Thuringia or some such place, and his Latin isn't very good. He is also getting paid by the page, and so works as fast as he can. He mistakes how much he can fit onto the parchment. His writing gets smaller and smaller as he nears the bottom of the page, and he begins abbreviating madly, making up contractions if he must. Where he cannot read a word he leaves a blank. By chance he copies out, say, *judex* on line 3, and when he turns back to the manuscript his eye falls on *judex* on line 7, and he accidentally picks up from there. The nib of his quill pen deteriorates, but he'll be damned before he cuts himself a new one. He finishes the work and goes back to Odo for his pittance.

Odo, meanwhile, has gone to the stationer to get a second *pecia* to be copied. The stationer has two copies of the commentaries on Lombard — it is the most widely used book on campus — and instead of giving Odo *pecia* 2 of copy A, he gives him *pecia* 2 of copy B. The stationer doesn't care. He is bored and surly. Besides, the copies are theoretically identical.

In fact, of course, each is riddled with its own distinctive errors. And so our impoverished undergraduate copies out *pecia*

2 of copy B and then perhaps *pecia* 3 of copy A, and so on through the entire work, splicing the two versions together. (This is precisely what happened to the fifty-three *peciae* of Aquinas's commentary on the *Metaphysics,* and the Dominicans at Catholic University have yet to sort it out.)

Twenty years go by. Odo's nephew (or perhaps his "nephew") is now at the university, and because manuscripts are precious things, the two copies of the commentaries on Lombard in the stationer's office are the same ones his uncle used. When young Odo rents it, it has suffered thirty years of wear and tear. Well-meaning know-it-alls have "corrected" the original. From careless handling, whole words and sentences have disappeared. The margins, as in any secondhand text, are filled with little prayers, jokes, drawings, and graffiti.

Odo, like his uncle, hires an indigent student who also makes a slipshod transcription of what is now an even more corrupt text. Most likely he will transfer the offhand marginal quips — "here I stopped," "damn the stationer" — onto his own copy, thinking them part of the text. Or he may be too bleary-eyed to care.

This goes on until the end of the fifteenth century, when the first printed editions of Saint Thomas's writings appear. At this point there exist about forty-five thousand manuscripts of his two dozen major works. They are scattered throughout Europe, for each scholar has returned home — to Valencia, Leipzig, York, wherever — with his "twenty bokes clad in blak or reed," like Chaucer's Oxford clerk. The genealogy is tangled, the quality bad. Still, all can trace their chromosomes directly back to Thomas.

Unfortunately, with the advent of printing, manuscripts become less valuable. Monasteries, now stocked with printed books, throw out their manuscripts or sell them off as scrap. Butchers use parchment to wrap up pork chops. Publishers use it to make bindings. ("Scratch the cover of a sixteenth-century book," Father Peter says, "and you will find a fourteenth-century manuscript.")

Wars, floods, and fires take their toll. Aristocrats hoard great collections, then die; the heirs call in an auctioneer to supervise the diaspora. Some manuscripts simply crumble into dust.

Now it is 1979. Perhaps 10 percent of the original stock of manuscripts has survived, some only as fragments. The task of the Leonine Commission is to reverse the process, to follow the clues back through time, to explore the tributaries in search of the source. Doing this for Aquinas's commentary on the *Metaphysics* has already taken the American section of the commission twelve years.

—◆◇◆—

In the bare, whitewashed editorial offices at Catholic University, Father William Conlan and another Dominican, Father Kenneth Harkins, spend their days hunched over a row of microfilm readers. On the screen: densely scriven manuscripts from the thirteenth, fourteenth, and fifteenth centuries. Magnifying glasses, red translucent rulers, and a century of accumulated experience suffice to pry loose their secrets.

The few shelves nearby sag with all thirty-two Leonine volumes published to date, along with select reference books: collections of Jerome and Augustine; nineteenth-century monographs on paleography ("Never confuse $\frac{i}{X}$ = *tenth* with $\frac{i}{X}$ = *Christ*," one of them warns cryptically); and several copies of Father Antoine Dondaine's masterpiece, *Les secrétaires de St. Thomas,* in which Father Dondaine not only argues that Thomas had a permanent staff of scribes but also identifies each of them by his handwriting — hand E, hand Q, hand A, and so on.

Methodical, silent, and intense, Father Harkins sits engrossed at his microfilm reader, dwarfed by its metal cowl, steadfastly deciphering a crude, gothic hand. (He does not suffer interruptions gladly.) There are seventy-four extant manuscripts of the commentary on the *Metaphysics,* nineteen fragments. (No autograph by Saint Thomas of this work exists.) Each must be checked against the others, line by line. Computers are useless. From

1949 to 1973, the IBM Corporation lent facilities and expertise in the compilation of the thirty-one-volume *Index Thomisticus,* a mammoth tabulation of precisely where and when Aquinas used what terms. (For example, he used the word *vis* and its inflections 2,540 times.) But a computer cannot make judgment calls, cannot determine whether *modū* is an abbreviation for *malum* or the ink has bled and it is really *modum.* Is it "evil" or "method"? Could make a difference.

From time to time, Father Harkins pauses to consult his copy of Capelli, the indispensable dictionary of Latin abbreviations. The first contractions were introduced in 63 B.C. by Tiro, a slave of Cicero's; the number swelled with the high cost of parchment in the Middle Ages. Many of them, such as *ꝝ*, *eꝫ*, and *ꝉꝫ*, verge on the hieroglyphic. The examination of a single manuscript page takes Father Harkins up to a day.

Editing the *Metaphysics* was probably a bad choice as the American section's maiden effort. On three occasions, friar paladins from one of the European sections, themselves hard at work on the *Questions on Evil* and other books, have made the transatlantic crossing to help out. Father Wallace spends much of his time just shuffling the lineup. "It's like being the Yankee manager at midseason," he says.

In his role as manager, Father Wallace has decided to scout out Grottaferrata and Rome, to untangle the commission's complicated staffing and finances. And in his role as embattled president he invites the press along.

—◆◆—

There have been five distinct stages in the life of the Leonine Commission. The first, or papal, period began on August 4, 1879, when Pope Leo XIII, Servant of the Servants of God, affixed a red seal to the encyclical *Aeterni Patris.* The letter commended to the faithful the study of Aquinas, paving the way for creation of the Leonine Commission several months later. The Dominicans had been lobbying the pope for a decade, spurred on by envy of the Franciscans, who in 1870 had been awarded their own papally backed commission to produce the complete works of Saint Bonaventure.

The first few Aquinas volumes were painstakingly done, though not up to modern standards. In 1886, Leo ordered the commission to drop everything and begin rapid publication of the *Summa Theologiae*, the most brilliant synthesis of Christian thought ever produced. Instead of demanding meticulous textual analysis, however, the pope instructed the editors simply to "correct" one of the standard printed editions of the work against several manuscripts in the Vatican Library. The Leonine editors were livid — the *Summa* deserved better — but helpless; the first four volumes of the work were rushed into print in six years, an achievement in speed unequaled by scholarship. (The four volumes must be completely redone.) Fed up, the Dominicans decided to go it alone. That was in 1892.

Now began the "classical" period, under three legendary editors, Fathers Peter Paul Mackey, James Lyttleton, and Constant Suermondt. They meted out the work neatly. Father Mackey, an eccentric Englishman, dealt solely with Saint Thomas's handwritten autographs. Father Suermondt, a careful, patient Dutchman, did all the collations — that is, established the text in cases where no autograph existed. And Father Lyttleton, an Irishman born in the shadow of Tipperary's Rock of Cashel, hunted down Thomas's sources.

It was a prodigious little group. Between 1892 and World War I, they produced eight volumes, including five good volumes of the *Summa Theologiae* and three volumes of the *Summa Contra Gentiles,* in many respects Thomas's most modern work, because it rests primarily on logic, not Scripture, and is addressed to Muslims and Jews, not Christians. The *Contra Gentiles,* expertly edited and glossed, was a sensation in the small Edwardian world of medieval letters.

Unfortunately, Fathers Mackey, Lyttleton, and Suermondt didn't train any successors, which resulted in what Leonine editors call simply the "period of misery." It lasted roughly from World War I (when work was disrupted entirely) through the end of World War II, and was presided over by Father Clement Suermondt, nephew of Constant. Essentially, Suermondt II worked alone, making do with reluctant draftees and friars on sabbatical.

He did finish up the *Contra Gentiles,* thanks to octogenarian Father Mackey, who obligingly survived until the work was done. Suermondt II then wanted to start work on something else, but now there was no one who could read Saint Thomas's handwriting. He decided instead to compile an index of all Leonine volumes published to date. For twenty years he did little else. "It was a stupid, stupid thing," says Father Gils, who recounts Leonine Commission history with a masochistic rancor. (It appears to be his only vice.)

After World War II the Dominicans elected a new master general, Father Emanuel Suarez. (The Dominicans have always had free elections. That and a federal system of monasteries have led to speculation that the thirteenth-century Dominican Constitution may have been used by the Founding Fathers as a model in 1787. Admittedly, more Dominicans than historians support this view.) Suarez summoned a half-dozen young Dominican friars to the Leonine Commission. A year later, at the order's general chapter, the Dominican Congress, Suarez obtained budget authority for expansion. Two sections were created, one in Canada, the other at the Convent of the Saulchoir, in Etiolles, near Paris.

By the early 1950s, the so-called French period was under way. Fathers Bataillon, Guyot, Gauthier, and Contenson were all at the Saulchoir. Father Hyacinthe Dondaine, *"le petit frère,"* was teaching there. For the first time in its history, the commission was up to fighting strength. Under the leadership first of Father Dondaine, then of Father Contenson, the project flourished. Father Dondaine, a fine scholar, gave the editors a true sense of method and purpose. Contenson, who took over in 1964, was a crack administrator. The son of a French general, Father Contenson pushed the Leonine Commission to produce eleven volumes in as many years, each volume as close to perfection as human works can be.

With Father Contenson's death, in 1976, the commission embarked on a fifth, as yet untitled period. Epochs do not always end abruptly, however, and in a way the French period lingers on at Grottaferrata, now home to the remarkably cohesive group of Dominicans who first came together at the Saulchoir — Fathers Bataillon, Guyot, Gauthier, and the Dondaines. Grottaferrata is the critical core of the Leonine Commission, if not its official center. It is the font of expertise, the reliquary of experience. As Father Wallace puts it, "It is where all the nuts are gathered in one place."

—◆◆—

Father Bertrand Guyot careens with his passengers out of Rome's Leonardo da Vinci Airport, hunched up, in black beret, over the wheel of an old Renault. He is adept on the horn, quick across the dividing line. Yet he is convivial, swiveling his neck while going around mountain curves. *"Ah, oui, oui, oui-i!"* he will say with excitement, turning his eyes back to the road just in time to avoid a nun walking up the hill. For a Frenchman, he is not a bad Roman.

Father Louis Bataillon sits beside him, unperturbed. Fathers Guyot and Bataillon have been a team for a quarter of a century, the one short, robust, the technician, the other tall, ascetic, the organizer. At the dawn of the French period, the two of them scoured Europe for manuscripts, microfilming page after page. Was there rumor of a cache in Fritzler? The pair would take off, Father Guyot at the wheel. In eight trips they studied seven thousand manuscripts in four hundred libraries.

We climb into the Alban Hills, a volcanic rim six miles wide, southeast of Rome. Inside the rim are the pocks of smaller peaks and craters. The friars' house at Grottaferrata, astride a pock, has a clear view down to Rome and the Mediterranean. To the south, the turrets of Castel Gandolfo, the pope's summer palace built over Domitian's villa, can be seen when the wind bends the cypress. To the west, the tower of Saint Niles, the eleventh-century church whose frescoes Stendhal so enjoyed, rises above the olive trees.

Cicero's villa and the ruined town of Tusculum crown hills to the east. (The citizens of Rome destroyed the town stone by stone in A.D. 1191.) Paved and polished, an old Roman road climbs to the summit still, and the earth to either side yields nuggets of marble to the plow.

Around the friars' house is a cluster of medieval farmhouses and a sixteenth-century villa whose giant wine cellars sheltered Resistance forces during the war. (It now houses the three nuns who cook and clean for the friars.) The house is shared by both Dominican and Franciscan priests — an unlikely combination. The two orders have been rivals for 750 years. Both are mendicant orders, both set up shop at the University of Paris in the early thirteenth century, and both soon rose to intellectual prominence. In the thirteenth century, competition for priests was so keen that several popes had to intervene to curb recruiting abuses. In subsequent years, the orders traded charges of heresy; both sides suffered casualties, including Thomas himself, briefly and posthumously, in 1277. Historians of the period remain partisan. As the neo-Thomist philosopher Etienne Gilson has noted, "The list of Thomistic propositions involved [in the 1277 condemnation] is longer or shorter according as it is compiled by a Franciscan or by a Dominican."

Technically, the Grottaferrata priory belongs to the Franciscans, and like the Dominicans, the Franciscans here are scholars. Some are editing the *Archivum Franciscanum Historicum,* some the writings of Peter Lombard and Alexander of Hales. They fled here in 1966 after the Arno spilled its banks and ravaged Quaracchi, their old priory and press outside Florence. Among the casualties: the library and hundreds of freshly printed volumes of the works of Saint Bonaventure.

At Grottaferrata, the library is on the ground floor but atop Mount Saint Anthony, 1,230 feet above sea level. "There is no danger of flooding," Father Bataillon points out.

The thirteen Franciscans were joined by seven Dominicans soon after they settled in. This was Father Contenson's idea, and he was diplomat enough to pull it off. (In addition to heading the Leonine Commission, Father Contenson was an aide to Cardinal Willebrands and the Vatican's liaison with the Jewish community.) Grottaferrata today is a thriving monastic settlement, one of the few communal experiments of the 1960s that has survived.

Even aesthetically, Contenson's experiment has worked well. The Franciscans dress in dark brown robes with stiff, pointed cowls, sandals, and white knotted cords around their waists. The Dominicans dress similarly but in wool of purest white, with two long strips of cloth, called the scapular, falling in front and back from the shoulders.

In the refectory, with its rough wooden chairs and tables, the friars stand facing each other before meals. At vespers, they take opposite sides of the small chapel and chant alternate Latin verses. There is a special give-and-take between the two groups, a natural balance. At benediction, for example, Father Contenti, the Franciscan prior, performs the privileged, sacred duty of holding the consecrated host, the body of Christ, aloft before his brothers. But the hymn that is sung, the "Tantum Ergo," was written by a Dominican — Friar Thomas Aquinas. At Grottaferrata, Saint Thomas is outnumbered but never far away.

The friars are usually up before dawn, well before the shrill crowing of farmyard cocks pierces the heavy wooden shutters. Mass is celebrated at sunrise. Then comes breakfast: raw eggs, fresh cheese, cappuccino, homemade bread. The friars eat quickly. Most of them have long been accustomed to having a psalm read aloud during meals; spoons must be put down with the last "Amen." After breakfast, they adjourn to their rooms to work. They are called together again at noon, for dinner and Latin prayers. It is a fine medieval meal: fresh lamb, spiced, roasted onions, and cabbage, served up by Father Contenti. (As paterfamilias, he doles out all food and prayer and signals the beginning and end of each meal with a little bell. On Sundays he passes out fresh napkins.) On the table is local mineral water as well as red and white wine, the latter from Frascati, the winegrowing town founded by the villagers who fled Tusculum in 1191. After coffee the priests wander in the gardens or relax with *L'Osservatore Romano,* the Vatican paper.

Following a siesta it is back to work. In the late afternoon there is a period of silence before the haunting ritual of vespers at dusk. (Aquinas, it is said, was once hurrying down a hallway, late for vespers, when a statue of the Virgin Mary in a niche suddenly spoke to him. "You're late," she reprimanded. "Shh," he shot back, "it's the hour of silence.") After vespers, a light supper, and then for some, more work, for others a bit of recreation or quiet prayer.

There is a sense of purpose and contentment at Grottaferrata that I have rarely seen before. At night an unearthly calm settles over the priory; surfeit and worry are strangers here, and an old gatekeeper bars disorder and trivia from the grounds. I ask Father Bataillon if he will be my Virgil the next day.

He laughs. "So you think this is hell?"

—◆◆—

The friars' house is built around a cloister where scalloped remnants of Roman columns hold up marble bench seats and red clay flowerpots. Because the complex is built into the summit of Mount Saint Anthony, there are in fact two ground floors. The chapel is on the lower of these, its windows overlooking the cloister on one side, the valley on the other. I serve Father Bataillon's morning mass, rain and wind beating against the stained glass, and then, after breakfast, we ascend to the other ground floor in a small caged elevator.

The French Dominican editors are masters of technique, and at Grottaferrata everything is at their disposal. A duplex library, its levels joined by spiral staircases, is stocked with anything a good medievalist could desire. Incunabula, books printed with movable type before 1501, squat side by side with modern paperbacks. In wire cases along the walls, handwritten manuscripts are kept under lock and key.

The heart of the scholarly effort is the *Sala Edizioni*. The room is filled with microfilm cabinets, ten units high, twenty units across, containing microfilms of the manuscripts collected by Fathers Guyot and Bataillon in the early 1950s — some 4,500 in all.

"The most beautiful manuscripts are generally the least useful," Father Bataillon explains as he pulls out a lavishly illuminated presentation copy. "Here is one done for the Duke of Urbino in the late fifteenth century. Although there were printed books at the time, he didn't believe in them. And here is one made for Pope John XXII, the pope who canonized Saint Thomas. He was old, so there are no abbreviations and the writing is big. Useless for our purposes, of course."

Everything is arranged according to the monasteries or libraries where they can be found, from A to Z. Fathers Guyot and Bataillon are now helping Father Hugues Shooner, a Canadian associate, compile Volume III ("Montserrat to Zwettl") of the *Codices Manuscripti Operum Thomae de Aquino,* an extensive catalogue of all the manuscripts in their possession. (Volume I runs from Admont to Fulda, Volume II from Gdansk to Montreal.)

"It is impossible to say where manuscripts will be found," Father Bataillon says. "We think we have 90 to 95 percent of all extant Aquinas manuscripts, but of course, by definition, there is no way of telling. We are sure only that we do not have all of them." Many have been arbitrarily divided into several parts, then disseminated as gifts to, say, Oxford, Vienna, Bologna, and Naples. It takes years to track down the sections. "All of these microfilms," Father Bataillon says, pointing to a separate file cabinet, "are of manuscripts listed in libraries as pertaining to one thing but also containing a portion of something else — specifically, a book by Aquinas." They have been discovered more or less by accident, much as if a browser in an open-air stall in Lagos were to stumble across a lost Fitzgerald short story stitched inside a Penguin edition of *Bleak House*. Manuscripts are always being found. Urban renewal has turned up whole libraries hidden by the French Revolution.

In an adjoining room is Father Guyot's microfilm camera (he has his own darkroom downstairs), a modern photocopying machine, and portable and cabinet-size ultraviolet readers for recovering the texts of soiled, erased, or "corrected" manuscripts. An ornate safe nearby shelters handwritten manuscripts, the commission's guinea pigs. Father Bataillon pulls out a small piece of scribbled parchment, one inch square. His expression is pained. "Here is a piece of Saint Thomas's handwriting," he says evenly. "Someone in the fourteenth or fifteenth century cut up many of his original manuscripts into little pieces like this as keepsakes for the devout. Typically, most of them are lost." Only about 10 percent of what Thomas is known to have written in his own hand has come down to us, to the infinite distress of the Leonine Commission.

—◆◆—

Reconstructing the presumed original text is never easy. If an autograph of Saint Thomas's exists, and if Father Gils can make sense of it, the job still consumes a decade. Generally there is only a fragment of an autograph or, more likely, none at all. At this point the editors must fall back on collation. The first ingredient is a working base text that serves, like the vanishing point in drawing, as an arbitrary reference point to bring the various elements into perspective. Usually the editors take a standard printed Latin edition of the work — the Marietti edition, say — and check it against four or five extant manuscripts, merging and purging where warranted.

This base text is then typed at the top of two-by-three-foot pieces of graph paper, one line per sheet. Notations for each surviving manuscript of the work under study run down the left-hand margin. Thus, Wr^2 would be the second manuscript in Wroclaw, Poland, the John of Frankenstein transcription; O^5 would be the fifth manuscript at Oxford.

The editor begins, for example, with Wr^2, checks it word for word, line by line, against the base text, and records all variations. He finishes several months later and begins on O^5. Soon he has something that looks like this:

Base Text:	*Hic*	*ponit*	*flagellationis*
Wr^2:	"	"	*flagellis*
O^5:	"	"	*flagelli*

Of course, the list may be one hundred or more manuscripts long, and this phrase merely one of tens of thousands.

Collating is relatively unskilled labor, requiring chiefly a sophisticated knowledge of gothic Latin and the boredom threshold of a toll collector. Interpreting the results and arranging manuscripts into the *stemma,* or family tree, requires a much defter hand.

There are always clues — often too many clues, as Inspector Maigret would say. By the time collation has been finished, several thousand variants will have been identified, each manuscript differing from the others by as much as 10 percent. After several years of close analysis, the patterns and relationships will begin to emerge.

Take the case of Aquinas's first book, the commentary on Isaiah. Only a quarter of the work exists in autograph; call it

A*. Beyond *A**, eighteen manuscripts are extant. Most of them bear a colophon, or inscription at the end, stating that they derive from an original transcription of *A** made by one Jacobinus of Asti, a secretary to Saint Thomas and the man Father Dondaine identifies as hand A. Naturally, the Jacobinus manuscript itself is lost, but let us hold its place and call it *a*.

Some thirteen of the manuscripts have clearly been copied from a single manuscript at the University of Paris stationer's office. (They have *pecia* markings, common pagination, and the folios begin and end with the same words.) The exemplar, labeled π, is also missing, but it can be roughly reconstructed from the consensus of its progeny. Since the progeny contain the Jacobinus colophon, π itself must have borne it. It is thus a child or grandchild of *a*.

The five remaining manuscripts, nonuniversity in origin, are from Bologna, Seville, Paris, Oxford, and Florence. Seville *(Sr)* and Paris *(P)* were copied from Bologna — the evidence leaves no doubt — and Bologna *(Bo)* bears the Jacobinus colophon. π and *Bo* are therefore collateral descendants of *a*.

Oxford *(O)* and Florence *(F)* are unique. Both display the colophon and so are also descendants of *a*. However, when compared with the surviving portion of the autograph, *A**, they are found to contain one hundred correct readings where no other manuscript has them. This means that *O* and *F*, though based on *a*, have been corrected against *A**. Since there are no correction marks on either manuscript, one surmises that it was actually a common parent, φ, now missing, that was corrected against the autograph. (Because much of the autograph is lost, this means that *O* and *F* can be relied on to fill in some gaps.)

It turns out that φ and π, when reconstructed, manifest hundreds of common variants not found in the Bologna branch of the family, sign of yet another shared parent, β — missing, of course. β is the final link with *a*. The reconstructed *stemma* thus becomes:

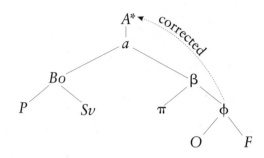

Every work of Aquinas tells a different story. In the *Isaiah,* this *stemma* happens to hold only for the second half of the book. In the *Metaphysics,* conflicting *stemmata* weave like DNA through every page. In the *Contra Errores Graecorum,* the mess begins with Thomas himself, who unwittingly used hundreds of quotations and citations from a forgery.

Once the *stemma* is established it is possible to reject most of the extant manuscripts as too corrupt, too derivative, or too distant, leaving a handful (*Bo,* π, and *F,* for example) that together will be used to correct the base text. The corrected text represents the closest possible approximation to Thomas's original. Restoration is finished.

Not so the work of the Leonine editors. They must still compose a long preface to the work, spelling out their method, carefully weighing all the evidence, recreating step by step the process of their reasoning. In short, the preface, which frequently runs to more than a hundred folio pages, complete with photographic plates, family trees, and fetching monographs on paleography, must justify the entire volume.

Footnotes must also be added, listing all possible alternate readings of the text. Thus, where the editors believe a proper reading to be *Balthasar,* they will nevertheless note that *Bo* reads *baldasar* and *F* reads *balcasall.*

The final and most specialized step is to sniff out Saint Thomas's probable sources. That job always falls to Father Jordan Peters and Father Albert Kenzeler, a two-man team headquartered in Rome. Father Peters is Dutch, but Father Kenzeler and Father Robvald Gallet, who is editing the *De Potentia,* are Belgian, part of a large Flemish contingent (including Father Cos in Washington and Fathers Gils and Deronne) on the Leonine Commission. Because they have chosen not to work at Grottaferrata, they are lodged at the Angelicum, a three-acre complex of churches, chapels, cloisters, cells, and lush vegetable gardens rising in terraces above the ruins of Trajan's Forum. Bernini's statue of Mary Magdalen touching the Christ hides inside the main church, which is open to the Leonine Commission but not to the public, like much else in Rome.

Most of the Angelicum was built in the sixteenth century. The lower levels, where broken columns pierce the floor, go back further. And no doubt there is older masonry beneath that. Rome is a baffling city. Recently, contractors pouring a foundation found they had greatly underestimated the amount of concrete required. They doubled the amount, but still there wasn't enough. Finally they discovered that the concrete was seeping into an uncharted catacomb.

Both Father Kenzeler and Father Peters are chain smokers, a reflection on their task. "Aquinas's sources are a real problem," Father Kenzeler says, puffing. "He cites Scripture all the time, of course. He cites the Church fathers — Jerome, Augustine, and so on. But he was not in the habit, to put it mildly, of giving chapter and verse. He is more likely to say something like 'As Simplicius says somewhere . . .'"

"Or," Father Peters interrupts, "he will simply say, 'As is noted in divine law.' Does he mean Scripture, or canon law, or the decretals, or what?" One citation from Augustine took two years to find. Sometimes the sources are so protean that not even Aquinas's contemporaries really knew what they were doing. One of Aristotle's books, for example, had survived down to the

Middle Ages only in Latin. Medieval scholars labored for years to translate it back into Greek. Decades later, translators vied to be the first to render it into Latin.

It takes people with a spelunker's sense of direction to tease out the facts. "I have a nose for *les sources,*" Father Kenzeler says with a shrug.

Despite a deep respect for the friars at Grottaferrata, the Flemings prefer not to share quarters with the French. The two nations have always had their differences. In 1297, King Philip was obliged to put the Flemish students at Paris under his personal protection. Animosity between French- and Flemish-speaking Belgians is a permanent feature of Belgian life. None of the Flemish editors, of course, admits to any feeling of personal discomfort; yet when out of earshot, each is willing to impute uneasiness to the others. "We are not in Grottaferrata," Father Kenzeler says, "because our resources are here in Rome. Of course, Father Gils is in Louvain because he prefers not to live with the French." Father Gils is equally frank. "Kenzeler and Gallet? I think they are tired of the French, no matter what they tell you. Me? I am simply too old to move."

Such feelings run just deep enough to keep the living arrangements separate. That done, the friars maintain a high level of mutual respect, cooperation, even friendship.

"It's astounding," Father Guyot will say of Father Kenzeler's nose for *les sources.* "I don't know how he does it." And everyone is quick to praise Father Gils. "But of course you must go to Louvain," one will say. Or, "I could explain, but Peter Gils is the real expert." Or simply, "Gils has just finished his preface to the *Questions on Evil.* We need someone to pick it up."

—◆◆—

My room in Louvain, at the Paters Dominikanen house, overlooks tiled, gabled homes of the kind depicted in the shop window Christmas displays on Fifth Avenue. Two streets away, the delicate clock tower of the town's great library rises above the rooftops. The Germans reduced it to rubble during World War I; it was lovingly rebuilt. It was bombed again during World War II; burghers still argue over whether Allied or German planes were responsible. Once more it was rebuilt.

The Dominican house, in the middle of the quaint, lace-curtained red-light district, is the only ostentatiously modern building in town. When the old monastery and grounds fell into decay a decade ago, the fathers decided to sell off most of the property and erect for themselves a vertical, modular structure of a kind the Japanese might admire. From the inside, fortunately, the building cannot be seen, and the roof provides a splendid view of what remains in many respects a medieval city.

Louvain also boasts the largest brewery in Europe (Stella Artois) and is the beer-drinking capital of the greatest beer-drinking nation on the continent. At the Dominican house, which appears to be one of the few monasteries in Belgium that does not market its own beer nationally, large bottles of local brew dominate the tables at mealtime, amid platters piled high with Belgian sausage and boiled potatoes.

The Dominican fathers rely on the tremendous resources of one of the oldest university towns in Europe. (Aquinas dedicated an Aristotelian commentary to the provost of Louvain.) The university is a center for Catholic priests who intend to follow an academic career; those hoping to rise in the Curia, the Vatican bureaucracy, generally study in Rome. In the eyes of the Romans, Louvain is a dangerous place. It is said that Louvain was working toward Vatican II while Rome was working on the Council of Trent.

Father Gils entered the Dominican order in 1930 after a rigorous stint with the Jesuits. His training was in Latin, Greek, and mathematics, and he is an excellent pianist. "I have a very logical mind," he admits. He also had no intention of joining the Leonine Commission. He had his eye more on pastoral work, on preaching. "I did not enter the order to produce texts," he explains. "I always thought the Dominicans were for people.

My superiors always thought they were for texts." His superiors ordered him to work on the Leonine project, however, and Father Gils took his vow of obedience — "my obedience," he calls it — seriously.

He took his Leonine work seriously, too. Living at the Saulchoir in the early days of the French period, he was appalled that no one on the commission since Father Mackey's death in 1935 had been able to read Saint Thomas's handwriting. "How could such a team of editors publish?" he asks, incredulous. So during vacations and after vespers he began to work on Thomas's autographs.

"You learn handwriting by reading it," he explains, "by reading, reading, reading, and making transcriptions yourself, by exploring *la physiologie du geste,* by trying to enter into the handwriting of the man. It is hard. Most of us cannot recognize our own handwriting from a few years back. Father Bataillon cannot read what he wrote yesterday. I spent eight years before I could do it properly. I read all of Aquinas's autographs, and I copied out the way he made every word. I determined the meaning of his word forms in ambiguous cases by figuring out that in certain other contexts, that form could mean only one thing. I put every word on an index card."

Father Gils is methodical, capable, opinionated. "Aquinas was a distracted man," he says. "He would not have been a good man to run the Leonine Commission. He makes so many little mistakes.

"Let me give you an example. In medieval dictionaries, it was customary to divide everything into opposites, good/bad, Christ/ Satan, and so on. Aquinas makes little Freudian slips all over the place. He writes things like 'All bad things come into the world through the sin of Christ.' He writes *priori* when he means *posteriori.* Sometimes he catches the little mistakes and misses the big ones. Sometimes he 'corrects' a mistake and makes it worse. But sometimes he really warms my heart. My favorite is

fragilitas
sed debilitas sexus feminei

In fact, he never finished writing *debilitas;* he wrote *debili-*, then crossed it out. *Fragilitas* is so much more appropriate for women, don't you think? *Fragilitas* is like a flower, *debilitas* is like a cripple."

The trouble with Aquinas is not so much his absent-mindedness as his handwriting. By all accounts it is the most difficult hand of the thirteenth century. "When Samarin taught paleography at the Ecole des Chartes," a medievalist and old friend wrote to me recently, "he was reputed always to give one page of the Master as part of the final exam. I find the story hard to believe, since few would have passed."

Gothic handwriting, unlike cursive handwriting, is written as a series of unconnected strokes. Thus, *dei,* the word for "of God," was written as ᚦᚲᛁ, five strokes. But Aquinas was a fast thinker; his writing trailed behind his thoughts. So he developed a kind of shorthand gothic. He wrote *dei* as ﹏, where the second stroke of the *d* is also the first stroke of the *e,* and the second stroke of the *e* leads into the stroke of the *i.* Similarly, Thomas reduced the normal gothic *g* from *ᵹ* to ᴇ. (The Aquinas *g* has long been a specialty of Gils's.)

The problem of penmanship, bad enough when dealing only with letters, becomes even more trying when words are involved. "In the *Isaiah,*" Father Gils points out, "there is a place where Aquinas has written ⟨glyph⟩, and every manuscript that we have — every one — interprets this as *u͡s canit,* which is the abbreviation for *ubi sic canitur,* 'where thus it is sung.' In fact, the whole thing should really be read *n͡ pcavit,* the abbreviation for *nisi peccaverit,* 'unless he should sin.'

"What happened? First of all, everyone mistook the *n* for a *u*, and then the *v* for an *n*, which happens even now. Typically, Thomas also misplaced the superscript *r*, making *verit-* into *-itur*. The *r* should have been over the *v*. But no. For Thomas, the movement from right to left is repugnant. He wouldn't go back that extra millimeter to put the superscript in the right place.

"Strangely, no one for seven hundred years thought twice about the error, because both readings make sense in context." He sits back, self-satisfied, and lights up a small cigar. "I was very pleased when I discovered this," he says.

The extent to which Father Gils has internalized Aquinas is extraordinary. He can write Thomas's hand as easily as his own. He can look at a manuscript and set the scene seven centuries ago. "Here is a draft by Saint Thomas. A secretary has been reading it over, and is having trouble, not surprisingly. See the check marks in the margin? These are places where the secretary — Dondaine identifies him as hand E, by the way — cannot read the writing, so he marks his place and saves his questions for Thomas. When Thomas explains, the secretary writes out the text in the margin.

"But wait. There is a second set of marks here. The secretary has inserted some entirely new words into the text. He is not just rewriting illegible words. What can this mean but that the secretary is reading back the text to Saint Thomas, and Thomas is making some editorial changes?"

It is late afternoon now, nearly time for the period of silence. I ask Father Gils what he thinks of Saint Thomas as a man, not as an exercise. He puffs slowly on his cigar.

"I love Saint Thomas," he says. "I know him through his handwriting. He didn't like writing, and he didn't like the method of argument he was forced to use — to use quotations from Scripture to make his case. Quotations are not proofs, and he knew it, and you know it, and I know it.

"Aquinas wanted to write another way, the way he wrote in the *Summa Contra Gentiles*. This is the work he loved the most.

How do I know? Because he worked on it for eight years. I see the book lying open on his desk all the time. I see him sitting down to it at his leisure, reading it, rereading it, correcting it lovingly over many years. This is not a book of quotations. There are almost none. It is a masterpiece of pure reason.

"But I love Saint Thomas most because he did not take himself seriously. Something extraordinary happened to Thomas. It was on December 6, 1273. It is said that he had a vision during mass. Some call it a nervous breakdown. Perhaps it is simply what happens to every man when he nears fifty. Of course, Thomas was nervous to begin with, nervous and impatient. Just look at his writing! But he had only one obsession: God himself.

"What happened on December 6? I think Thomas realized that nothing he had written had ever — could ever — penetrate the mystery of God. He never worked again. Several of his books end abruptly. And he died three months later. I love Saint Thomas especially because he stopped writing."

It has started to snow, and a light dusting covers the rooftops. The lighted clock tower of the library strikes 5:00 P.M.

"So when you see Father Wallace," Father Gils says, "you can tell him I am not a Thomist." He smiles briefly. "Or put it this way: tell him I am as much a Thomist as Brother Thomas."

—◆◇◆—

Flying back to the United States, I open up a book of limericks Father Gils has given me. ("Most of them are risqué," he warned.) Somewhere over the Atlantic I chance upon this:

> A crusty old monk was thought odd,
> For he labored at Latin unshod.
> When his friends asked him "Why?"
> He proclaimed with a cry,
> "For the honor and glory of God!"

—◆◇◆—

AUTHOR'S NOTE: I received a long letter from Gus Wallace in April of 1994, bringing me up to date on the work of the Leonine Commission. Though the commission struggles as always with a shortage of money and personnel, publication of new critical editions in Latin of the works of Thomas Aquinas continues. A number of the scholars I wrote about have retired from the commission, Gus Wallace being one of them. (He serves still as a professor emeritus at Catholic University, and he teaches a course in the philosophy of science every semester at the University of Maryland.) A number of other scholars mentioned in "All the Pope's Men" have died and are perhaps now conducting *disputationes* in the company of Aquinas himself. The departed include Fathers Del Pozo, Kenzeler, and Peters, and the two Fathers Dondaine. But Fathers Gils and Deronne, in Louvain, remain active, as do Fathers Bataillon, Gauthier, and Guyot, at Grottaferrata, and as does Father Conlan, in Washington, D.C. Some of the commission's vacancies have been filled by new recruits from the ranks of the Dominican order in the United States and Poland. The director-general of the Leonine Commission is an American, the aptly named John Aquinas Farren, O.P., who was once a student of Gus Wallace's. Three Leonine volumes have been published since my visit (*Quaestiones disputatae de malo, Sententia libri de anima,* and *Sententia libri de sensu*), one is now being set into type *(Sententia libri metaphysicorum),* and another will soon go to press *(Quaestiones quodlibetales).* Work has been undertaken on virtually all of the remaining volumes of the projected sixty-five-volume edition.

Gus Wallace concluded his letter to me with these words: "Considering the state of the intellectual life in the Church, and the loss of manpower (and womanpower) in the Order, it is an ongoing miracle that the Leonine Commission does as well as it does. In 1983 I attended a Galileo conference in Cracow, and fortunately was able to address the Dominican students who were studying there. That awakened interest in the commission, and is the proximate stimulus to our recruitment there. But if the director-general does not keep active and keep 'beating the bushes,' the chances for the future are not very bright."

My own feeling is that the commission will, as it has for more than a century, live up to Virgil's dictum: *Possunt, quia posse videntur.* That is to say, "They can, who think they can."

IV

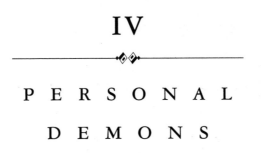

PERSONAL

DEMONS

They're Back

—◆◆—

THE LITTLE DEVILS

I DECIDED not long ago that it was time to catch up with the rest of America and get myself a personal trainer. I might start slow, with someone who would come into the office for an hour every day, and work myself up toward a full-time live-in trainer named Jake, who would help me to realize my full potential as a physical specimen. No sooner had I made this decision than my newfound ambition wilted, when it became apparent that personal trainers are hopelessly quaint and passé. The big thing now, to judge from news reports I see almost every day, is to have a personal demon — or, better, several of them. In the nation's expanding service economy, personal demons are the real workhorses, and they perform an impressive variety of tasks.

They make good chauffeurs, for instance. An article I remember reading about Michael Deaver, reporting his claim to be an alcoholic, explained that the former adviser to President Ronald Reagan was "driven by personal demons." The picture of Deaver that accompanied the article showed him, as if by way of proof, sitting in the back of his limousine. Thomas Wolfe, John Dos Passos, and Erskine Caldwell all had personal demons at the wheel, according to an article in the *Washington Post,* though Ernest Hemingway, as William Faulkner was quoted in the same article as saying, "wasn't driven by a private demon." Personal demons will go anywhere. Writing in the *New York Times,* Anna Quindlen talked about herself and her husband "struggling with a relationship, sometimes flying off with our own personal demons." The *Chicago Tribune,* noting the improved performance of the pitcher Fernando Valenzuela, explained that he was no longer being "chased cross-country by personal demons."

Personal demons do not always have it easy. At the Wimbledon lawn tennis championships a few years ago, John McEnroe was seen by a *Chicago Tribune* reporter "swearing at personal demons and giving innocent ballboys an earful." Another newspaper account described the U.S. downhill skiing champion Moe Johnson as "fighting injuries and personal demons."

Personal demons can give as good as they get. One press report noted that Pete Rose, as manager of the Cincinnati Reds, "was unable to beat his personal demons as consistently as he had generations of pitchers." Some personal demons apparently plague several people at once. The *Washington Post* observed that the outfielder Eddie Murray, who at the time was playing for Baltimore, was "not alone among old Orioles in choosing owner Edward Bennett Williams as his personal demon."

Along with professional athletes, people in government service are prominently possessed. When Robert S. McNamara, the former secretary of defense, testified during the lawsuit brought against CBS News by General William Westmoreland, the *Washington Post* pictured him trying to "wriggle loose from his personal demons." George Bush and Robert Dole found themselves in a similar situation immediately after the 1988 Iowa caucuses. The two GOP front-runners, according to *Time* magazine, "went into a defensive crouch fending off their personal demons." Pat Buchanan, who was for several years the director of communications in the Reagan White House, seems to be a Washington rarity: "He's entirely without any of the personal demons that so often occupy the men in power," according to the Reagan speechwriter Anthony Dolan, as quoted in *Time.*

Envy, gluttony, lust, covetousness, sloth, pride, anger — these are the Seven Deadly Sins, and for a good while now human beings have been trying to explain them away in the language of psychology and sociology. Now we are back to demons, which have not figured significantly in the Western world for about three hundred years. The writers of the texts introduced above probably don't mean to refer literally to a representative of Satan when they use the word *demon*, but they do mean to refer to some maleficent exogenous variable, for which a demon stands in as a kind of stuntman.

Nobody knows, of course, when a belief in demons as tormentors and inducers to sin first arose. The Judaic literature doesn't make a big deal about demons, though they do appear from time to time. The notion that demons are a powerful and pervasive influence in the affairs of men was mainly a Christian contribution, and it raised a lot of questions. Are demons the pagan gods? Are they fallen angels? Did God create them, and if so, why? The early Church fathers and medieval theologians had to grapple with such questions because they involve the very nature, and the source, of evil. From Augustine to Aquinas, philosophers labored to construct an elaborate demonology.

And yet, ironically, it was not during the Dark Ages but during the Renaissance and the Enlightenment that the fear of demons and their human agents reached its height. Charlemagne in the eighth century forbade the burning of witches, regarding it as a pagan custom. The laws of King Coloman of Hungary in the eleventh century took no notice of witches, "since they do not exist." Only with the dawn of the age of science did an awareness of demons and their earthly wiles become, as H. R. Trevor-Roper argued in a famous essay, an "explosive force" and "a standing warning to those who would simplify the stages of human progress." The lesson seems to be that there is something about a society whose smug self-conception is one of rationality and sophistication that leaves it wonderfully open to the forces of unreason.

Trevor-Roper's observation may have relevance in our own

time. Certainly the popularity of personal demons seems of a piece with the age. To have a personal demon is at once an assertion of individuality, a denial of responsibility, and a claim on sympathy. That combination is a potent one, and it prolongs a great deal of disagreeable behavior. You've got to give the devil his due.

Dear Me

DO YOU HAVE an office job? If you do, does a lot of mail
land on your desk every day? If it does, is a large portion of that
mail from people you don't know? If it is, do a lot of those
people, instead of addressing you in the salutation as "Dear Mr.
Surname" or "Dear Ms. Surname," address you as "Dear Fore-
name Surname" — "Dear John Smith"?

Quite a few of them do, I'll bet. Where I work, which happens
to be at a magazine, one letter out of every four that arrive
addressed to a specific person and that come from someone
unknown to that person begins with a forename-surname salutation. Let's be clear on this point: the "Dear John Smith" at
issue is not the tactical "Dear John Smith" — the one that serves,
after a cordial and sufficiently extensive correspondence, as a
hint that the gulf between courtesy title and first name is ready
to be spanned, the one whose function is similar to that of an
arm moving with studied carelessness to the back of the car seat
occupied by a date. No, the "Dear John Smith" I'm thinking of
is the one penned by a complete stranger, the one leveraged on
the assumption that intimacy is but a small, inevitable step away.
I have been asking friends in lines of work other than my own

if they encounter this formulation with any frequency, and they have each replied, in essence, Yes, now that you mention it.

I bring the matter up not simply because it represents yet another small incursion of the outside world into the battered preserve of the self — yet another indication of how many of the gentle and perhaps even wise social conventions developed during the past million years or so have in the course of a generation been breached or dismantled — but also because it begs for understanding. Why has it become so common to begin letters in this way?

One possibility is that epistolary etiquette has been infected by the technology that enables billions of computerized letters to be sent out with the space after "Dear" simply filled in with the addressee's name as it appears on whatever mailing list is being used. Another possibility is that many Americans reach adulthood without ever having learned the basic rules of conducting a correspondence. The program director of secretarial science at a college in Boston was strongly of this opinion. She fairly threw up her hands when I described the phenomenon I was looking into. "So many people just don't know how to write a proper business letter," she said. A third possibility is that having to use "Mr." or "Ms." seems impossibly quaint to people who have come of age since roughly 1965 (although one would think that the atavistic "Dear" might also seem a little ridiculous). Most of today's social tendencies, according to this view, are urging us toward greater familiarity and informality, even at the risk of seeming insincere, self-conscious, or odd. The consequences are on display everywhere; one medical technician was quoted recently in the *New York Times* as saying to a patient on a gurney, "Hello, my name is Tim, and I'll be taking your CAT scan."

I have no doubt that these larger forces contribute to a climate in which a salutation like "Dear John Smith" can flourish, but I also suspect that something else is at work — indeed, has been the primary catalyst. There is only one situation in which any published manual of style that I've consulted either proposes or is willing to countenance the use of a forename-surname salutation: as the authors of the *Katharine Gibbs Handbook of Business English* (1982) explain, "If it is not possible to determine the gender of the addressee, omit a courtesy title in the inside address and in the salutation." The Katharine Gibbs manual goes on to give the example "Dear Meredith Riker." *The New American Handbook of Letter Writing* (1988) likewise endorses this practice, giving the examples "Dear M. J. Shell" and "Dear Leslie Gowan." Certainly most of us have at some time been confronted in writing by an ambiguous Courtney, Lindsay, Robin, or Shawn and had to guess at the person's sex — and guessed wrong. "Dear Lindsay Wagner" or "Dear Robin Leach" offers a safe and sensible way out.

Are unisex names now so common that the stylistic device invented to cope with them is making inroads beyond its sanctioned domain? Several recent conversations with experts in the field of anthroponomastics — the study of people's names — give reason to believe so. Leonard Ashley, a professor of English at Brooklyn College and the author of the book *What's in a Name?*, says that people born during the past few decades are far more likely to have unisex names than people of earlier generations and that the trend is accelerating. This development can be traced, he says, not to any major change in the names that boys are given but to a quiet revolution in the naming of girls.

Two things have been going on. First, female babies have been given once unambiguously male names in such large numbers that droves of these names — for example, Tracy, Stacey, Jody — are now considered unisex. (For that reason they are somewhat less likely in the future to be given to male babies.) Second, female babies are increasingly being given as forenames the kind of surnames, often family names, that males have been getting all along — Montague, Fairleigh, Brennan — and that have no inherent gender content (and may have no relation to the baby's own family). Professor Ashley says he hears repeatedly from parents that they have given daughters genderless names so that as the girls grow up, they can "better compete with men," at least insofar as the competition is waged with résumés, applications, and other written documents and communications. Many parents also believe that women who do not have exclusively feminine names will be deemed by others to be more competent than women who do. (These same rationales have been encountered among parents of daughters by another specialist in anthroponomastics, Ralph Slovenko, a professor of law and psychiatry at Wayne State University.) The ascendance of unisex names is being reinforced by their predominance among the names for female characters in soap operas and elsewhere on television. According to Professor Ashley, now, more than ever, the names of characters in movies and television programs influence name selection of every kind.

As it becomes more and more difficult to tell the sexes apart on paper, I fear that trying to hold the line on "Dear Mr." and "Dear Ms." will become untenable. One can imagine, of course, a variety of initiatives that could help preserve gender distinctions and thus the use of courtesy titles in salutations. In some cultures male and female names, no matter how similar in essence or provenance, are differently inflected: Aleksandr and Aleksandra in Russian, for instance. Perhaps we could adopt something along those lines. Or perhaps some sort of typographical convention might be devised to distinguish female and male versions of the same name: !Marion and ?Marion, say. The problem with both proposals is that the erasure of distinctions, not their preservation, is precisely what many people want.

There is ample precedent for government intervention in the matter of names — a footnote in a scholarly paper by Ralph Slovenko some years ago cites several of them, including the measures adopted in Argentina in the 1880s to help ensure the assimilation of large numbers of Europeans — but nothing of the sort is conceivable in the United States. Neither, I expect, is the hale British manner of salutation ("My dear Holmes"), which dispenses with gender and title altogether yet achieves a blustery dignity nonetheless.

I will not be surprised, then, if within the next few decades we emerge into a world in which business communications either are curt memos or begin with the forename-surname salutation, a world where "Mr." and "Ms." survive mostly in speech (though not in every social class) and maybe for a while on envelopes (as when a couple shares a last name). It may be that in the end "Ms." will slightly outlast "Mr." as a courtesy title, if only because mizzes tend to outlast misters, but it will surely begin to atrophy as soon as its opposite number is gone.

I feel a momentary sense of loss whenever, in collections of letters, I meet up with a Johnsonian "Sir" or a Dickensian "yr. obdt. svt." It is painful to watch as other serviceable conventions of long standing prepare to join them. It is painful, too, to realize that I, far from being part of any solution, am because of my name one small part of the problem.

Hostage

—◈◈—

FIVE DAYS A WEEK I arise punctually at 6:15 and after a frugal repast set out for a train that comes for me at 7:34 and completes its journey at 8:04, whereupon I walk the three blocks to work. At 12:25 I go to a club for some exercise, returning at 2:00. I leave the office at 5:55 to catch a train home, and after driving a lonely route that never varies, I walk in the front door a few minutes after 7:00. This is the behavior, I was recently informed, of a man who has forgotten Abu Nidal — of the kind of person terrorists would describe as user-friendly.

"Vary your times and routes of travel": that advice and a lot more came the other day in a piece of mail from the Defense Information Access Network, of Rancocas, New Jersey, which has published a booklet called *How to Avoid, Prepare For, and Survive Being Taken Hostage.* The study is drawn from various unclassified State Department publications, and it is truly comprehensive, with sections devoted to such matters as Personal Preparations ("Update your will"), Residential Security ("Be alert to persons disguised as public-utility crews"), Transportation Security ("Be especially alert in underground garages"), and Torture and Pain ("Many people find that they can tolerate much more than they thought they could").

It is a chilling document in some ways, and not only because I own a Japanese car ("Avoid using vehicles that identify you as an American"). The real source of concern lies in the subtext, in the bland and matter-of-fact dissection of the psychology of dominance and submission. I don't live in Beirut or pay much attention to security arrangements, but reading this booklet made me realize that hostage-taking incidents are impossible to avoid in daily life.

The occasion may at first seem innocent enough — say, taking a seat next to a stranger at the outset of a long journey. Suddenly the stranger begins to talk. "The moment at which a person is captured, no matter where that capture may occur — in the home, in an automobile, in an airplane, or in the office — is psychologically traumatic. You may be suddenly transformed from a relaxed and complacent frame of mind to a state of absolute terror." Telephone calls from people who want to sell you something, such as insurance or financial planning services, are an insidious and increasingly common form of hostage-taking, even in neighborhoods otherwise considered safe. These calls are sometimes difficult to terminate. "Interrogators will also know what you fear most. They may know, for example, that one of your primary concerns is for the welfare of your family, and they will play upon this fear to induce you to talk." Day after day thousands of people are held in long lines against their will by a faceless few who operate inside most government offices and at all ticket counters, and who probably control the fast-food industry. "Their activities are intended to make you more compliant. . . . They may, for example, . . . keep you in an unsanitary environment, dehumanized by being called by a number." Many virtual abductions occur in doctors' offices, where victims are forced to strip and then made to sit in a chilly room, waiting helplessly. "The best reaction . . . is to concede that the terrorists have the upper hand, and that resistance would be futile and dangerous. . . . Escape may be possible, but it requires an unlikely combination of events."

In their own ways and for their own purposes, my children take me hostage several times a day, although usually without violence. "While they may make life unpleasant for you, they are unlikely to do anything intentionally that is life-threatening. Dead, you are worth nothing to them." As a result of these episodes at home, I have come, somewhat to my surprise, to appreciate and even depend on the so-called Stockholm syndrome — the little-understood phenomenon whereby "hostages become emotionally involved with their captors" and "occasionally, the hostage-takers reciprocate the positive feelings of the hostages." It may be that in a world where hostage-taking of one kind or another is a pervasive and licit social gambit, the Stockholm syndrome represents not a form of aberrant behavior but a powerful force for cohesion. Around my house, anyway, the casualties have been light.

The Right Wrong Stuff

—◆◇◆—

BEGUILING

BLEMISHES

I RECALL SEEING a poster many years ago for an appearance by the guru Mahara-ji, who advertised himself as the "fifteen-year-old perfect master." On the poster a passerby had written, "When I was fifteen, I thought I was perfect too." I am not fifteen, and I have not thought of myself as perfect for years. Indeed, for quite some time perfection has not even been a personal objective. When a new year commences, I no longer resolve to terminate any of my dreary vices. Rather, I think about how, at some perpetually future date, I might upgrade the quality of my imperfections. Perhaps I am making a virtue of necessity, but it seems to me that having a flaw or two is usually preferable to having none.

There is a difference, of course, between a gross defect and an attractive blemish. For a deficiency to be winning there must exist a certain level of adequacy. The mistake supposedly woven into every Oriental rug, on the grounds that only Allah is without flaw, would serve no purpose (and have no cachet) if the carpet were defective throughout. The very finest shortcomings call attention less to themselves than to the estimable context in which they occur.

I know a woman, an American, who has become fluent in Uzbek, a Central Asian tongue; owing to the origin of her tutors, however, her Uzbek is marred by an Afghan accent. The failing compels respect. As it happens, I have a long wish list for flaws of just this kind. Were it possible without effort, I would like to speak an easy French whose textbook precision was occasionally interrupted by lapses into crude Corsican patois. I would like to bring to the piano such technical virtuosity that I occasionally undermined a composer's intentions. I would like to be reproached in chess circles for a style of play "overly imitative of Capablanca." I would like to have a broken nose, badly healed, that suggested to others how unbearably handsome I would otherwise be.

I cannot lay claim to defects so fine as these. Up to a point, however, imperfections are worth fostering even when they do not, in Goldsmith's phrase, lean toward Virtue's side. If nothing else, they confirm that what one lacks in common with the Supreme Being, one holds in common with the highest of his creations. It is important, somehow, that even Homer nods, and that we all know it. Imperfections of a middling kind contribute to comity. By making tolerance necessary, they also make it possible.

This is worth bearing in mind with respect to New Year's resolutions, lest in our zeal we be tempted to go too far. All of us manifest shortcomings from which others derive solace or satisfaction. A rush toward perfection on even a modest scale would be uncharitable as well as disruptive. But cultivation of the right *wrong* stuff is another story and can only be encouraged. "She did make defect perfection," Shakespeare wrote of Cleopatra. That, on a more modest scale, is my very goal. A gruff manner concealing inner warmth, a smile shaped by a hint of tragedy, an utter self-control except in the presence of fools or smoked salmon — these are some of the refinements that I hope to introduce in the twelvemonth ahead. At the very worst, the endeavor will end in noble failure.

Misfortune's Catalogue

—◆◇—

A   W E E K L Y

W A R N I N G   O F   W O E

There shall no evil happen unto thee: neither
shall any plague come nigh thy dwelling.
Book of Common Prayer

UNTIL RECENTLY, those words were my belief and conso-
lation, and I passed a placid few decades on the planet fearing
not the pestilence that walketh in the darkness nor the sickness
that destroyeth in the noonday.

To be sure, I endured my share of the usual maladies, and even
an operation or two, but the afflictions always ran their course
— "resolved," as the medical journals would have it. I was not
obsessed with the fecal coliform count of my drinking water and
never wondered whether the source of that water might be a
spring surfacing within a fenced hog lot. I considered roughly
nil my chances of contracting otitis from *Pseudomonas aerugi-
nosa* in a mobile redwood hot tub. Pruritic rash and occasional
urticaria associated with gypsy-moth caterpillars did not concern me, nor did Siamese-cat-borne tularemia, nor renal disease
caused by the naphthalene in mothballs. I did not insist, as of
course I do now, that foreign exchange students be swabbed
with Betadine and don antiseptic gauze masks should they wish
to make my acquaintance.

I was shaken from complacency by a little magazine called *Morbidity and Mortality Weekly Report,* which is published by the Centers for Disease Control, in Atlanta. For reasons I have been unable to establish, a few years ago the publication began arriving at my office, addressed to me by name. The etiology of the subscription matters little, however. The fact is, no other journal has so quickly commanded my attention and earned my respect.

This may come as a surprise to those who have only skimmed an issue or two at the county morgue, for the publication lacks the slick appeal of *National Geographic, Country Life,* and other standard waiting-room fare. A typical issue of *MMWR,* as the magazine is familiarly known, consists of sixteen pages — six inches by eight and one-half inches in size, the paper nonglossy, the type sans serif, the ink black. The editorial demeanor is brisk and businesslike, redolent of competence and devoid of levity. The gray text is enlivened only by tables and charts. These, however, are formidable instruments, and they tend to reinforce the average citizen's reluctance to "become a statistic." That, at least, is my experience.

There is always one table listing the number of deaths (by cause) in 121 U.S. cities during the previous reporting period. Another records the incidence of "specified notifiable diseases." From my second issue I learned that in New York City alone there had been eight reported cases of leprosy during one ten-month period. Nationwide, there had been nine reported cases of plague, all bubonic or septicemic and not, thank heavens, pneumonic, of which only one case has been diagnosed in this country since 1925. By presenting such data in the same format week after week, for city after city, the editors betray their confidence that mankind's most dreadful complaints (and, therefore, the magazine itself) are in for a long run.

The real appeal of *MMWR* to a layman like me — most of the journal's 54,445 subscribers are physicians doing front-line duty — lies less in its admirable accretion of statistics than in its feature stories. Three or four of these appear in every number, bearing titles like "Niacin Intoxication from Pumpernickel Bagels — New York," "Food-Borne Illness due to Inadvertent Consumption of Marijuana — California," "An Outbreak of *Pseudomonas* Folliculitis Associated with a Waterslide — Utah," and "Contamination of Potable Water by Phenol from a Solar Water Tank Liner — Georgia." Because the editors avidly solicit "accounts of interesting cases, outbreaks, environmental hazards, or other public health problems" from their correspondents around the country, the menu is delectably varied.

A dentist in Charlottesville, Virginia, writes to report an alarming rate of tooth enamel erosion among competitive swimmers in his care — the result, it is learned, of acid concentrations 100,000 times the recommended level in a local pool. Following a Colorado blizzard, Denver hospitals report fourteen snow-blower-related amputations, the casualty in most instances being a single (male) finger, usually the middle digit. In Puerto Rico, Florida, Texas, and New York, doctors are surprised to find seventy-seven refugee Haitian males developing breasts, possibly owing to a hormone imbalance brought on by the victims' suddenly improved diet. In California, public health officials recount the aftermath of an attack by a single rabid dog in a Yuba County parking lot: seventy people received antirabies prophylaxis, two thousand dogs were vaccinated, and three hundred cats and dogs had to be destroyed. The total cost came to $105,790.

The *Weekly Report* is quite high on rabies, and, I might add, rightly so. One survey in the early 1980s noted that "documented rabies in animals [has] doubled in the last three years" and warned particularly of an increasing incidence of the disease among domestic dogs and cats. After a case of bovine rabies was diagnosed in Pennsylvania, the warning was extended to cows. (The animal, which had been infected by a bat, was "subsequently euthanized.") A few months later, *MMWR* passed the word that the epidemic was radiating outward from its epicenter on the West Virginia border at an unusually fast clip: "approximately 25–50 miles per year."

That rate, I reflected, would bring the frothing creatures to my doorstep — not far from Boston — in just a few years. The prospect of hundreds of raccoons relentlessly trekking northward was enhanced a few issues later by another report, "Epidemic Typhus Associated with Flying Squirrels," and the subsequent realization that any ground attack would inevitably have air support.

One unusual characteristic of the writing in *MMWR* is its high caliber. The editors achieve a crisp, lucid, oddly vivid style suggestive of Hemingway as retold by Strunk and White. Each summary, like the affliction it describes, has a precisely defined beginning, middle, and end. Satisfied that the facts will carry the story, the editors do not play games. One article begins: "On April 28, 1981, a 35-year-old man was seen in a Modesto, California, hospital emergency room for nausea, vomiting, dark urine, and jaundice. He reported contact two–three weeks earlier with an ill friend who had 'yellow eyes.'"

Given the nature of *MMWR*, where no news is good news and there is never no news, even the most innocent of topic sentences conveys an atmosphere of grim foreboding. "On June 27, 1981, a 17-year-old American arrived in Kenya as an exchange student. . . ." The veteran subscriber need read no further to envision the boy on a shimmering tarmac in Nairobi, suitcase in hand, a putrid haze of exotic pathogens misting his epidermis, the pores obligingly dilated by heat for easy penetration. Sure enough, the lad has a date with Chlorquine-resistant falciparum malaria (from which, after suitable agony, he recovers).

Judging from the frequency of the phrase's appearance in *MMWR*, I have the impression that "*something*-resistant" is a kind of Bronze Star (with oak leaf cluster) that has been earned by all too many of the planet's least law-abiding microzoa. During the past few years I have encountered multi-resistant *Salmonella,* Methicillin-resistant *Staphylococcus aureus,* Spectinomycin-resistant *Neisseiria gonorrhoeae,* Dapsone-resistant *Mycobacterium leprae,* and an abundance of other noisome pathogens that seem capable of resisting everything except a potential host ("host" being *MMWR*'s euphemism for *me*).

But there are many doors to let out life other than those held open by microscopic predators. Indeed, the journal's periodic winter survey of hypothermia episodes and carbon monoxide intoxication, as well as its occasional warm-weather roundup of reports from selected local coroners (e.g., "Aquatic Deaths and Injuries — United States," a regular summertime feature), provide a refreshing change of pace. From time to time the *Weekly Report* will also pause to celebrate a medical landmark — the centennial of Robert Koch's discovery of the tubercle bacillus, say — or to remark the progress of some worldwide cleanup effort, such as the Diarrheal Diseases Control Program. But the magazine's editors are clearly happiest when they have a mugging to report: a case of assault by viral or bacterial agents, preferably abetted by chains of coincidence.

In a Texas home, a mouse is trapped and killed in the bathroom. Within days, five family members, infected by *Rickettsia typhi* in the feces of the rodent's fleas, come down with murine typhus. In New Mexico, a thirty-one-year-old man awakens to discover his cat savoring a rabbit under the bed, is bitten as he attempts to deposit both outdoors, and four days later develops "fever, rigors, myalgia, non-productive cough, pleuritic pain, and vomiting." In California, a fifty-six-year-old woman bakes a commercial beef pot pie, puts it aside on a kitchen shelf when her husband unexpectedly comes home with a bag of takeout hamburgers, returns to it after two and a half sweltering days, devours it on the spot, and contracts botulism.

To this last report *MMWR* appended an Editorial Note to the effect that heat-resistant (needless to say) *Clostridium botulinum* is latent "in many fresh, frozen, and other food products." The editors speculated that the initial baking had "killed competing organisms in the [pie] and eliminated much of the oxygen." Left out at "incubator-like temperatures," the spore-forming anaerobic bacteria were able to germinate with abandon and secrete their lethal toxin.

The sad truth is that eating accounts for about half of all episodes of illness or death featured in the *Weekly Report*. And to judge from the recent outbreak of psittacosis among turkey processors in Ohio (not to mention the asthmalike illness that winded crab processors in Alaska), even proximity to foodstuffs can be sufficient to bring on rash, fever, cutaneous vasodilation of the face and trunk, and sometimes death. Animal or vegetable, processed or fresh, cooked or raw, comestibles of every variety are best given a wide berth.

This is particularly advisable if the provender has been prepared by what *MMWR* (with ill-concealed contempt) calls a "food handler." We are all, I expect, familiar with the type. Lie in wait outside a restaurant bathroom and you will often see him emerge, wiping his hands on a soiled apron, ready now to shred the iceberg lettuce or cough into the *crème anglaise*. "Suspected Hepatitis A in a Food Handler — California": in the *Weekly Report*, items like this are commonplace; only the details vary.

Consider the case of one food handler, an unwitting carrier of *Salmonella typhi*, who worked in a tortilla *molino* in San Antonio, Texas. Into his gloveless hands each morning came not only cornmeal to be shaped into tortillas but also *barbacoa* to be deboned. (The *Weekly Report* defines *barbacoa* as "salted, unspiced cow head cooked overnight under steam pressure.") Over an eight-week period, this food handler spread typhoid fever to seventy-two of the *molino*'s patrons. According to *MMWR*, this was the largest "common-source" outbreak of typhoid fever since 1973, when more than three hundred workers in a migrant labor camp in Florida succumbed.

Yet, to be fair, food handlers are sometimes only convenient scapegoats. This was forcefully brought home to me by the *MMWR* report "Interstate Common-Source Outbreaks of Staphylococcal Food Poisoning." According to the editors, picnic lunches supplied by a single catering establishment in Allegheny County, Pennsylvania, sidelined fourteen travelers on a bus in Iredell County, North Carolina, one day in July; thirty-three people attending a picnic in Grove City, Pennsylvania, the next day; and fifty-one people on an Ohio River boat trip from Pittsburgh to Waterford Park, West Virginia, two weeks later. As it turned out, responsibility for the outbreaks lay not with the caterer but with a Brooklyn, New York, supplier of Cryovac-packaged hams, whose "cold smoke" method of processing permitted "exposure to bacterial growth temperatures for over six hours." The distributor ultimately repossessed thirty-six thousand pounds of tainted gammon.

One expects this sort of thing from meat, of course, but the prevalence of *Yersinia entercolitica* among vegetarians in Washington State suggests that a flesh-avoidance posture is only the first step toward an effective program of disease deterrence. In all, eighty-seven cases of gastroenteritis in Washington in the course of one typical year were found to have been caused not by spoiled meat but by "a locally produced brand of tofu, an oriental soybean curd, packed in untreated spring water." Seventeen people were hospitalized and one underwent a partial colectomy. Upon investigation, sanitary practices at the tofu plant, where the employees used an outdoor privy and observed "poor personal hygiene," proved questionable.

The weak of will may be tempted to shrug off *MMWR*'s warnings about food. But only the foolhardy will ignore the evidence in the *Weekly Report* about other countries. To put it bluntly, foreign lands, along with their products and their peoples and probably their cultures, must be inherently malignant. The sensible person will eschew physical contact with all of the above.

The evidence from *MMWR* on this matter is, unfortunately, conclusive. A Little League organization in a "southcentral Pennsylvania community" buys 2,928 seven-ounce bags of cashews imported from Mozambique, sells them in the stands, and then watches the bleachers empty as fans go home with "poison ivy-like dermatitis." Black pepper imported from Brazil infects 126 people with *Salmonella oranienburg,* an infrequent visitor to the developed world. Forty-five people in Washington, D.C., are felled by gastrointestinal illness after sampling Marcillat brie, made in France.

The journal is filled with reports of travelers acquiring Katayama syndrome (an acute form of schistosomiasis) after rafting on Ethiopia's Omo River; of infants from Calcutta spreading salmonella among their adoptive American families; of U.S. airmen, fresh from Korea, imparting new and puissant strains of gonococcus to stateside affiliates; of dengue fever in a forty-one-year-old man returning from India and the same in a fifty-four-year-old Hispanic male "with a history of travel to Puerto Rico." In an Editorial Note on this last case, the editors attributed a recent increase in epidemic dengue activity in part to the growing frequency of air travel. Jet aircraft, they wrote, provide "an ideal mechanism for dengue virus movement between world population centers."

Not surprisingly, what is good for dengue is also good for measles. *MMWR* once linked eighty-nine cases of measles in Ulster and Dutchess counties, New York, to a student who had recently traveled to the Soviet Union with his high school class. This lad's feat was soon surpassed by that of a fourteen-year-old Dade County, Florida, youth who, while vacationing in Latin America, "had face-to-face contact with a cousin in Peru who had fever and a generalized maculopapular rash." Upon the boy's return to the United States, he exhaled with every breath a disease-laden effluvium that went on to infect 203 people in fifty-seven different schools, four day-care centers, one community college, and a military academy.

For all its merits, the *Weekly Report* seems to fail in one important respect: never does it give its readers any general advice about how, in the face of what is clearly an unrelenting assault, to protect life and limb. The editors do provide explicit solutions to specific problems: Avoid contact with dead rodents. Keep irrigation pipes away from electric power lines. Stay away from silos freshly filled with corn. Don't use mothballs as an air freshener. Ventilate the indoor firing range. Other precautions can be inferred: Decline cream-filled pastries on cruise ships. Turn away door-to-door prostitutes. Wear a face mask when swimming in sewage. All such advice is well taken. But the editors have shrunk from distilling their thousands of sensible injunctions into a handful of lifesaving tips.

Perhaps, upon reflection, that is as it should be, for any such tips would likely prove as reliable as those of a racetrack tout. While the journal could reasonably counsel the health-conscious to avoid flora, fauna, and food, along with air, aliens, and anything aquatic, the determined few adhering to this regimen might yet be crushed in their sleep (cf. "Hospital Bed-Associated Deaths — Canada, United States") or run over by a reaper (cf. "Farm-Tractor Associated Deaths — Georgia"). No, the editors of *MMWR* are not given to self-delusion. In their stoic refusal to promise panaceas, they acknowledge the proficiency of caprice and the feebleness of our deterrent.

Type B, A-Wise

—◆◇◆—

A F A S T L I F E I N

T H E S L O W L A N E

People with Type-A personalities — those uptight, compulsive, competitive, aggressive, sometimes hostile, insecure overachievers — can greatly reduce their chances for a heart attack by modifying their behavior characteristics, according to a study by San Francisco physician Dr. Meyer Friedman and Stanford Prof. Carl Thoresen of the School of Education. . . .

Driving in the slow lane instead of the fast lane, stopping at a traffic light when it turns yellow, lingering at the dinner table, standing in the longer rather than shorter grocery lines, speaking more slowly, and learning to smile more at strangers were a few of the exercises tried.

item from the
Stanford University News Service

SATURDAY. ARISE, AS is my habit, at 5:15 A.M. Listen to news in course of sixty bench presses, a hundred sit-ups. Translate two of Horace's epodes into Urdu before scanning the *Examiner* and the *Chronicle, Dow Theory Forecasts, Value Line Investment Survey.* Brush teeth in shower. Down diet pill with instant espresso. Sort mail on porta-desk while . . . doggone it, she did it again. Second time since giving notice. Compose terse memo to maid on which way toilet paper should unfurl (blind carbon to wife). Turn roll around. Same damn story. Want something done right, got to do it yourself. Ticks me off. Already 6:20, and books still uncatalogued, *Economist* unread. "Slow down, you move too fast,/You got to make the morning last." Words of song somehow percolate into sentience as I shave. Point conceded. Foot off the pedal. Deep breath, count to ten — o . . . 1 . . . o — urgently taking binary shortcut. Doesn't work, still revved up. Maybe Doc Friedman right after all. Maybe time to road-test some pacing drills — win one for the ticker.

Switch at once from brace of Norelcos, deployed on both jowls, to single Wilkinson Sword blade. During 273 seconds this adds to task recall that Wilkinson Sword helped carry day at Omdurman, Kandahar. (Norelco, *maybe,* was at Grenada.) Don trousers one leg at time, soon get hang of it. Feel better already. Serene, resolute, join spouse for usual repast of Tang and Toaster Tarts. *La plume de ma tante est dans le jardin.* Only seductive drone of Berlitz lesson disturbs morning stillness as we eat.

Resolve to linger for ten minutes after meal. Linger, linger, linger, linger, shred a napkin, tap a finger. Ever notice how mind slips into rhythmic rut during arbitrary waste of time? America is back, America is back. Or, worse, "Winchester Cathedral." Linger, moreover, starting when? When *I* finish? When *wife* does? What if there are houseguests? Produce Heuer stopwatch and measure interval between first cleaned plate (mine, at 7:13:26.4 A.M.) and last (hers, at 7:24:53.9), determine midpoint (7:19:10.15), and calculate ten-minute period from there (can get up, in other words, four minutes, sixteen and one-quarter seconds after wife puts down fork). Set egg timer. In ensuing restorative interlude can almost hear mitral valve murmur thanks. Heartbeat downshifts gratefully into theme from *Hawaii Five-O.*

Ping! Time's up. Next stop, supermarket. Direct route exists to store from home, no signs or signals. Chart course instead through twenty-six traffic lights, four "all way" stop signs. Opportunity, now, to brake for amber, practice relaxation skills. Tough snaring yellow light when you need one, even knowing synchronization pattern. Always arrhythmias in timing cycle. Keep having to wait at green. "All way" stop signs more reliable. Rule of road: first car at intersection gets right of way, other vehicles follow, counterclockwise. Here I exercise wholesome restraint. Let seven full cycles go by before asserting legal rights. Good place, by the way, to return phone calls while paying bills or, better, take time to smell the flowers (keep bunch within reach on passenger seat). Bad time, though, for (honk!) *Die Schreibfeder meiner Tante* (honk!) *ist in dem Garten* (beep-beep!). In occluded roadway to rear, restive motorists bleat a path to Infarct City. Heart goes out to the bastards.

On to supermarket for time-absorption therapy. Grocery list organized so no two consecutive items will be found in same aisle. Doesn't work out perfectly, needless to say. Always a slip somewhere. Turns out Tylenol next to the QT, antacid across from the Bisquick. Blessing in disguise, frankly. No choice now but suddenly to "remember" something never meant to buy — gosh, left off Belgian endives — and perambulate to produce before turning back to Tums. Time filling shopping cart expands to one hour, fifty-eight minutes, exceeding estimate. Automated arterial hypertension monitor near checkout gauges systolic blood pressure at 190. Big plunge since breakfast, but room for improvement. Won't give up till down to zero.

Checkout time. Question: which line at bank of counters is really longest? Is "longest" same as "slowest"? Checkout line metabolism exceedingly complex. Store size, day of week, line length, cart volume, checker speed, payment method — only a few of twenty-seven identified variables. Embolism appears unpredictably, brought on perhaps by out-of-town check, unpriced foodstuff. Just as suddenly clot may clear.

Decide to leave nothing to chance. Divide purchases into several carts, nine items or fewer in each. Go through so-called express lane, always congested, as many times as needed (eleven) till shopping done. On each sortie insinuate baffling items into carts of customers in front, prompting further delays. ("Hey, hold it, whoa! Where'd those endives come from?" "Sorry, sir, I've already rung them up.")

Ideal time, I discover, to smile at strangers, fore and aft. Less a smile, actually, than a lips-sealed, corners-piquantly-upturned conveyance of guarded bonhomie. Result confirmed in pocket mirror. Exhibit fifty-seven smiles in all, of which twenty-one, unfortunately, are returned. Median artery reveals pulse rate idling at ninety-eight.

Take interstate home, winding up workout with lap of slow-lane prophylaxis. Enveloped on highway by feeling of great calm, inner peace. Should have inaugurated new regimen years ago. Teeth grind softly as I savor prospect of quality time with son, home for weekend from preschool. Been clamoring to learn how to snap a paper clip, cheat at cards. Got to pull up those A-minuses first. From behind, siren's screak overtakes rich Slavic sonorities on tape cassette. Ease onto shoulder. "Do you know how fast you were going?" Ручка тёти в саду. *Repeat after me.* Ручка тёти в . . . "Turn that thing off. Do you know how fast you were going?" Smile number fifty-eight, not returned. Of course I know. Twenty-three and two-tenths miles per hour. Двадцать три и две десятых. A speed you can live with.

Make sure to record benchmark in MemoMaster. Next time out must trim back those tenths. Courting another ticket, of course, but I'll fight that one, too.

A Blaze of Glory

—◈◈◈—

THE   HEARTBREAK

OF   SHC

"ALREADY THE SNOWS have scattered and fled," the poet Horace wrote in one of his odes, "already the grass comes again in the fields and the leaves on the trees." What Horace neglected to mention, though he was probably as relieved about it as I always am when spring rolls around, is that the end of winter also marks the end of the traditional peak season for spontaneous human combustion.

I am your average sensible, nonsmoking, appropriately insured sort of fellow who nonetheless is drawn to headlines in the tabloids like "Preacher Explodes During Sermon: The Most Bizarre Case of Spontaneous Combustion Ever!" and feels compelled to glance through any illustrated book with a title like *Unsolved Mysteries of Science*. I was sixteen years old when, flipping through such a volume, I first encountered the case of Dr. J. Irving Bentley, ninety-two, of Coudersport, Pennsylvania, who was found (actually, whose unburned slippered foot was found) by a gas-meter reader in December 1966. The balance of Dr. Bentley had apparently been reduced to cinders after burning a hole in a bathroom floor and falling into the basement. Nothing else in the house was harmed. Photographs were taken of the bathroom scene — the hole, the foot, the metal walker resting askew against the bathtub — and they remain seared, so to speak, in my memory.

Some three hundred instances of alleged spontaneous human combustion have been reported during the past three hundred years, and the consequences, if not the causes, have in many of these cases been reliably described. The distinguished Dutch surgeon D. De Moulin noted several years ago, in the medical journal *Archivum Chirurgicum Neerlandicum*, that many of the accounts handed down through the centuries were written by reputable physicians of unquestioned integrity — indeed, by physicians "well known for their scientific contributions to medicine." These include, for example, Claude Nicholas Le Cat (d. 1768, "in his day the most renowned lithotomist in France") and Bradford Wilmer (fl. 1779–1802, "who at the time enjoyed a reputation for his treatment of goitre with burnt sponge") — men, in other words, in whom one is inclined to place implicit trust.

The first instance of spontaneous human combustion that survives in the professional literature was discussed by the Danish anatomist Thomas Bartholin in 1663, in *Acta medica et philosophica Hafniensia*. Bartholin reported the case of a woman in Paris who had long enjoyed her brandy and who one night "went up in ashes and smoke" as she slept, apparently achieving an extreme temperature yet doing little damage to any part of the adjacent domestic environment, including the straw mattress upon which she slept.

Subsequent accounts of spontaneous human combustion are more or less consistent with that one. A few stray extremities aside, the victim is always totally consumed, flesh and frame. The coroner usually remarks a sweetly fuliginous smell at the scene and is utterly baffled by what has occurred, having never seen anything like it in all his years as a medical examiner. The setting is usually somewhere inside a house, often the bedroom, but spontaneous combustion has reportedly claimed victims in cars and on boats and city streets; one woman, after dancing all night with her fiancé, "suddenly glowed with blue flames and was reduced to ashes," according to a newspaper account. The most typical casualty, students of such incidents contend, is elderly, overweight, and female; the victim's typical vice is a taste for alcohol; and the time of death is typically during the holiday season. While this does not exactly place me, or others similarly situated, in an at-risk group, enough exceptions have been documented to suggest that none of us is necessarily apyrous.

Spontaneous human combustion used to be accorded the respect it clearly deserves. It was *the* wrath-of-God affliction during the eighteenth and nineteenth centuries — meted out, some believed, to punish intemperance — and accounts of its visitation advance the plots of many old novels, most famously Charles Dickens's *Bleak House*. A lot of ingenuity has been invested over the years in possible explanations. I favor the eighteenth-century idea, which is that the friction caused by particles in the bloodstream bumping into one another creates a certain animal heat, or *ignis elementaris,* which, upon surpassing a certain threshold, requires only a *causa occasionalis,* such as bourbon, to touch off a conflagration — highly localized, to be sure, but fraught, potentially, with extreme personal significance. Other explanations have implicated a buildup of combustible gases, the explosive properties of human emotion, the influence of geomagnetic fluctuations, and the presence of a subatomic particle, yet to be validated, called the pyrotron. Despite a diminished measure of public concern about the issue, there are still quite a few theorists out there (prey, of course, to factionalism) subjecting SHC, as they call it, to serious, or at least sincere, scrutiny. Like other covens of specialists, they have their own newsletters and magazines, their own *guerres de plume,* and their own repertoire of terrible puns.

Is there really such a thing as spontaneous human combustion? I have consulted doctors at several leading burn centers around the country, and their reactions amount, in effect, to "Pshaw" (a word that, by the way, I have only seen in print and have never in all my life heard spoken). I received such responses as "I have no knowledge of a valid basis for the concept of spontaneous human combustion" and "Based on my own experience as a burn surgeon, I think it is highly unlikely that this is a reliable phenomenon." Question these men and women more closely, however, and you will discover that their real quarrel is with the word *spontaneous,* in the discredited sense associated with "spontaneous generation" (remember Needham and Spallanzani?). Yes, they say, bizarre, inexplicable, radically self-contained immolations do from time to time occur. But no, there exists no rogue chromosome or genetically transmitted pyrotron; nothing inherent in the constitution of any representative of *Homo sapiens* can cause him or her, without provocation, to burst unilaterally into flames. Rather, SHC is simply the capricious consequence of various combinations of rationally explainable if unpredictable exogenous events, one of which happens, sometimes mysteriously and unaccountably, to provide ignition — the strike of an errant bolt of lightning, say, or a wafting ember from the hearth, or a brush with a sweater that went through the dryer without StaPuf. Instead of something that could happen to anyone for a very specific reason (a reason, perhaps, that might one day be vitiated through genetic counseling), human combustion is actually something that could happen to anyone at any time for any reason under the sun.

But not usually, it seems, from April to October. It was, I suspect, this benign interval to which Horace was referring when he advised, "Now is the time for drinking, now the time to beat the earth with unfettered foot."

Busy, Busy, Busy

A M E R I C A ' S

S P A R E - T I M E   E T H I C

IN SEARCH of a telephone number and an address recently, I flipped through a new edition of the three-volume *Encyclopedia of Associations;* when next I looked up, an hour or so had gone by. With its twenty-three thousand densely crafted entries, the *Encyclopedia of Associations* is an absorbing and indispensable reference work. It is also a monument to the United States as the world's leading nation of joiners. We like to think of this country, of course, as one of rugged individualists, and perhaps it is. But it is also a place where people need only the flimsiest hint of a shared interest to clump together like iron filings on a magnet. As Tocqueville and other observers have noted, there seems to be no activity, endeavor, condition, passion, peeve, or state of mind in America that lacks an institutional base to rally the faithful and carry the torch.

My own accomplishments in this respect have been very modest. At a young age I was a member of a fan club built around the Blackhawks comic-book series, my secret identity (I can now reveal) being that of "André." I have for some years been a member of the American Automobile Association, but the only meetings I attend involve tow trucks. In looking through the encyclopedia, I came to understand that my appreciation of America as a nation of joiners was extremely limited and largely abstract. I realized that I had little idea of the vast number of ways in which Americans, workaday demands behind them, deploy their energies and their time.

I decided to spend a day calling up some of the associations listed in the encyclopedia. My criteria for selection came down mostly to curiosity.

—◆◈◆—

An advocate, I learned, can be found for almost anything, and advocacy is one of the three broad categories into which the associations I encountered tend to fall. Joe Anne Ricca, who was until recently the president of the American branch of the Richard III Society, answered the phone at her office in Hackensack. She was quick to come to the defense of the generally vilified British monarch. Ricca contends that Richard's evil reputation was largely the creation of Tudor propagandists. (Henry VII, Richard's successor, burned the work of everyone who had anything good to say.) She pointed out that x-ray analyses of various portraits of Richard III show them to have been overpainted in order to magnify the size of the hump on his back. She questioned the implication of Richard in the famous murder, in 1484, of the two princes in the Tower, his young nephews and rivals for the throne, arguing that there are other plausible suspects and that it is even possible that the princes escaped to the continent. The Ricardians, seven hundred and fifty strong, publish a journal and sponsor scholarly research. They believe that they may at last have turned the tide.

Seaver Leslie, an artist who lives in Wiscasset, Maine, believes

204 • J U S T   C U R I O U S

that another tide may have turned. Leslie founded and for nearly two decades has been the director of Americans for Customary Weights and Measures. As the name suggests, the purpose of the group, which has fifteen hundred members, is to halt the encroachments in the United States of the metric system. The group's post office box number in Wiscasset is 5280, which is, of course, the number of feet in a mile. Its newsletter, *The Footprint,* appears twice yearly, on the summer and winter solstices. Leslie observed during our conversation that traditional measures — the inch, the foot, the mile, the furlong — are all somehow derived from human proportions or human activity. The furlong, for example, was the distance a plowman could walk from home and still be within earshot. Can it be coincidence, Leslie asked, that the rungs on ladders the world around, from culture to culture, are all a foot apart? Traditional measures, he said, "touch the poetic soul of every individual in America." In contrast, when it comes to metric, people can't even agree on which syllable to stress in the word *kilometer.* Leslie's free time is spent lobbying for the repeal of Public Law 100-418, the Omnibus Trade and Competitiveness Act of 1988, which enshrined the metric system as "the preferred system of weights and measures for U.S. trade and commerce" and requires the U.S. government to begin using the metric system in all its operations. He noted that metric has been beaten back three times — in the 1870s, the 1920s, and the 1970s — and is confident that it will be beaten back again.

Leslie's nemesis is the American National Metric Council, an association with a hundred and fifty members, most of them corporate, based in Bethesda, Maryland. The council's president is John Deam, who in his professional life is the director of business operations for a company that designs laser-based measuring instruments. Deam talks in even, logical tones. He, of course, holds Public Law 100-418 in high regard, and believes that once private industry comes around, the public will follow quietly and inexorably. He notes in metric's defense that it is easy to comprehend the relationship of, say, centimeters to meters, whereas there is no such self-evident relationship between feet and miles, or between inches and yards. He wonders what it says about this nation that at a time of an increasingly integrated world economy the United States stands alone among industrialized nations in resisting the metric system. But Deam is heartened by some recent developments. As of last year, for example, the General Services Administration has been accepting new specifications for federal buildings only in metric units. For the record, the American National Metric Council does have an official position on the pronunciation of *kilometer*: accent on the first syllable, not the second — a position, I suspect, that will be as congenial to many Americans as the metric system itself. Asked, by the way, whether he uses a yardstick at home, Deam replied, "I'm afraid I do."

—◆◇◆—

A second category of associations consists of what might loosely be called contestants. I spoke with Tom Cabot, of Hermann, Missouri, who is the president of the National Organization of Mall Walkers, a group established "to give national recognition to people who walk in malls for exercise." The organization sells log books so that its one thousand members, most of whom are women above the age of fifty-five, can record their mileage, and it awards patches and pins to those who achieve certain distances. Cabot, who sells sports medallions and Christmas ornaments for a living, explained that mall walking is related to the German tradition of outdoor "Volks marching." In 1979 Cabot helped organize the American Volkssport Association and sought to recruit the people he saw walking in malls. He founded the Mall Walkers because "I couldn't get them out."

In Scranton, Pennsylvania, Bob O'Leary picked up the phone at the American Armwrestling Association. O'Leary, a distributor of nutritional supplements, is the executive chairman of the association, which has two thousand members and is affiliated with the World Armwrestling Federation, headquartered in Calcutta. (Arm wrestling is India's second most popular sport, after soccer.) O'Leary explained that there are two styles of arm wrestling, stand-up and seated, and that arm-wrestlers are known as "pullers." Arm wrestling tournaments are held somewhere in America every week of the year. Any major issues facing the arm wrestling community? "Drug testing at national events," O'Leary said. Also, a lot of effort has gone into lobbying for arm wrestling's inclusion as an Olympic sport — "obviously long overdue."

Larry Kahn, of the North American Tiddlywinks Association, in Silver Spring, Maryland, explains that most of the hundred American dues-paying "winkers" in his group are men and that most have a background in the hard sciences. In the United States, major tiddlywinks tournaments are held four or five times a year. NATwA has a sister organization known as ETwA, in England; of English winkers, Kahn observes, "They're even nerdier than we are." Like participants in many other sports and games, winkers have developed a distinctive jargon. They may say, for instance, "I can't pot my hurdled wink, so I'll piddle you free and you can boondock a red." Tiddlywinks apparently enjoyed something of an efflorescence in the United States in the 1960s and 1970s, after which it entered a period of mild decline. Kahn blames this on the nation's having experienced a time of cynical economic opportunism and creeping spiritual discontent, which together eroded the bedrock of silliness upon which the edifice of tiddlywinks is erected. Or so I inferred. Actually, what he said when asked about the cause of the decline was simply, "Reagan."

—◆◆—

Finally there are the collectors. The world headquarters of the International Sand Collectors Society is located in Old Greenwich, Connecticut, and I spoke with its president, William S. Diefenbach, a retired management consultant. Diefenbach explained that the membership was held together, as it were, by "a common bond of sand." Sand from the beaches of Normandy. Sand from Mount Saint Helens. Sand from the "break-

through point" of the Channel Tunnel. Sand from the sand traps
of famous golf courses. (A golf course division of the society is
in the planning stages.) The society has four hundred members,
Diefenbach said; General Norman Schwarzkopf, the commander of Operation Desert Storm, was granted honorary membership (which he accepted). Asked about recent activities, Diefenbach said, "We recently had a sand swap" — the first such event
in the United States. Diefenbach puts out a newsletter, *The Sand
Paper,* which among other things describes "the surpluses and
needs of individual members." The members clearly don't want
for projects to keep them occupied. Some items from the newsletter: "Bert Brim sent a supplement to his catalog of Ocean
Beach Sands, bringing the number up to 830." "Angela Maure
is back from holiday in Egypt, and offers you: Desert al Rayum,
Hurghada, the Valley of the Kings (Karnak and Hatscepshut),
and the small island of Magwish." "Warren Hatch has made a
superb 58 minute VHS tape of 42 sands seen through a scope
at 10 and 20x."

The man who answered the phone at the number listed for
the International Carnivorous Plant Society was Leo Song, its
business manager and also the manager of the greenhouse at
California State University, in Fullerton. He explained that the
purpose of the society, which has seven hundred members, is
"to provide information that concerns carnivorous plants, from
care and culture to taxonomy, nomenclature, political action,
and the dissemination of new hybrid names." Asked what draws
people to collecting carnivorous plants, Song said, "When you
think about plants eating bugs, it kind of turns the tables."
Asked about the disturbing reputation of the Venus's-flytrap,
Song called it ridiculous. "With the plants we've discovered so
far," he said, "you don't have to worry about your cat getting
eaten — even with genetic engineering." He added, though, that
when people ask him if dangerously carnivorous plants do exist,
he always tells them, "Well, there are areas out there that have-
n't been explored."

Danny Perez, a union-licensed electrician in Norwalk, California, would surely agree. Perez, too, is a collector, in a way. He heads the Center for Bigfoot Studies, whose purpose is to obtain a specimen of the large, shy, primatelike creature that is believed by some to inhabit the northern woods. He was inspired to take up the cause, to which he devotes all his spare time, by the movie *The Legend of Boggy Creek,* a documentary about Bigfoot that he saw at the age of ten. Apparently the Bigfoot community, which consists of several hundred people, is divided on strategy, the division being between the take-it-alive camp and the shoot-to-kill camp. Perez favors the first approach. He conceded, however, that the second would be "a lot safer."

—◈◈—

All told, I got in touch with about twenty-five associations, and at day's end it was hard to shake the feeling that compared with the lives of the people I had been talking to, my own was rudderless. Lifting my sights, I also began to wonder whether there must not exist an umbrella association to which people who run associations can belong — an organization that offers advice on, say, publicity and fundraising, or on holding conventions, and that perhaps lobbies the government for various kinds of tax exemption. In the Washington, D.C., phone book I found something called the American Association of Societies and Organizations, but despite repeated attempts was unable to get through. Were the lines being tied up by urgent calls from the American Fancy Rat and Mouse Association? Professional Psychics United? The Antique Doorknob Collectors of America? The United States Amateur Tug of War Association? The Marx Brothers Study Unit? The Flying Funeral Directors of North America?

What I know is that according to the taped message, "all of our staff are busy." I don't doubt it for a second.

V

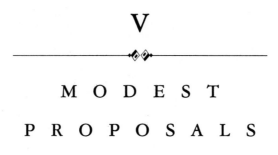

MODEST
PROPOSALS

Novus Ordo Seclorum

—◆◆—

S A N I T Y

S A V I N G   T I M E

WE HAVE REACHED that time of year, with the winter
festivities finally behind us and the drear of February to the fore,
when the people I know tend to concede privately what we
ought to acknowledge publicly: that our system of holidays,
established willy-nilly over the course of two centuries, is in a state
of disrepair. Some of our holidays — Columbus Day, Washington's Birthday, Memorial Day — have become unmoored not
only from their traditional dates of observation (by act of Congress, so that they can be welded into three-day weekends) but
also from any real substance. For most people, they are little
more than days off. Other holidays — Thanksgiving, Christmas,
New Year's Day, Martin Luther King Day, Presidents' Day —
are bunched too close together. One passes them like kidney
stones and is overcome, in late January, by the relief of pain
suddenly abated. No, the system that has evolved is not one that
a sensible nation would invent. And while Americans are not
always a sensible people, there are a few corrective steps that
even we might take.

Let's first recognize the few holidays that function properly:
Easter/Passover, the Fourth of July, Thanksgiving, and Christ-
mas/Hanukkah. No one tinkers with the dates on which they

fall, and everyone pays at least lip service to each holiday's intrinsic high purpose. They are engaging in other ways. The Fourth of July and Christmas, being affixed to specific dates, fall on different days of the week in successive years, offering variety in the holiday configurations. How glorious it is when the Fourth falls on a Tuesday or a Thursday, inviting a four-day weekend. Easter and Thanksgiving, for their part, though affixed to specific days of the week, roam across the calendar like shortstops, sometimes playing in, sometimes on the edge of the far grass. Passover and Hanukkah are more unpredictable still, varying from year to year both by date and by days of the week. All these holidays have a strong ritual component that transcends commercialization. Two of them, the Fourth of July and Thanksgiving, are the occasion for sporting events of the most appealing kind: the daylight double-header and the high school football game. There is nothing not to like about these holidays.

They stand in sharp contrast to New Year's Eve, which is an occasion of hollow cheer and fake bonhomie and comes too hard upon the heels of Christmas. The start of the new year is in any case misplaced. Psychologically, the new year begins not on January 1 but on September 1, and we should adjust our calendars accordingly. Of course, Labor Day would then be too close to New Year's, so let's move it to the first Monday in October, and let's have the following Tuesday be the new day when income taxes must be paid. The proximity of tax day to Labor Day could hardly be more appropriate, and many of us could use a long weekend before the filing deadline. (The World Series should start that weekend, too.) Having to pay taxes in October would, admittedly, leave us feeling a little poorer in December, but that might be to the good.

With New Year's moved out of the way, relieving some of the congestion, Martin Luther King Day could stay where it is, on the third Monday of January. I admit to being pleasantly surprised by Martin Luther King Day, which in the short period of its official existence has been observed with high-mindedness and dignity. But it is wispy; it lacks a certain heft. That problem could be solved by arranging for the final National Football League playoff games to be held on the Saturday and Sunday directly preceding it. Martin Luther King Day's relative stature would be further enhanced if we canceled the Super Bowl, which is rarely as good as the playoffs and is in any case grotesque. (The playoff winners could simply flip a coin.) Finally, Martin Luther King Day needs some sort of familial or collective rite. Perhaps it could be a day devoted to good works on the community's behalf, when nobody rests until dinner.

Moving on: Memorial Day should be kept as a holiday, but it needs some refurbishing. Do most people stop for very long on Memorial Day to contemplate what this observance is actually about? Or is Memorial Day just an excuse to go lie in the sun? We all know the answers to those questions. That's why Veterans Day should be moved back from November to reinforce its martial cousin, and why the pair should be celebrated together, on the first rainy day after the last Sunday in May. Fixing the date to a rainy day has several advantages. It means that the holiday would be observed on different days in different parts of the country, and would serve, therefore, as a symbolic bulwark against encroaching homogeneity. It means that communities would often be taken by surprise as they awoke of a morn — a delightful prospect. And it means that the Memorial Day parade would be sodden — a mild yet effective reminder that military service is no day at the beach.

Presidents' Day is a joke, and so is Columbus Day. By now the only thought given to Lincoln, Washington, and Columbus on the holidays meant to honor them is how to use images of their faces to sell merchandise, chiefly linens and underwear. The two holidays should be disposed of at once.

Taking the places of Presidents' Day in February and Columbus Day in October would be a calendrical innovation, loosely based on daylight saving time, called sanity saving time. It would work like this. Every February, on a day to be selected randomly

— perhaps by giving Dr. Joyce Brothers an opaque jar holding twenty-seven black marbles and one red one and asking her to pick out one marble each February morning on the *Today* show — the date would suddenly spring forward by a week. If Dr. Brothers picked the red marble on February 9, for example, the day would instantly turn into February 16. A week's worth of obligations would disappear — and what is more, February would pass 25 percent faster than it does now. Adults would be given the option of not counting any missed birthdays, and children could reschedule theirs for any day they chose. Similarly, on a randomly selected day in October we would fall back by a week — on the twentieth, say, we could suddenly find ourselves on the thirteenth again — and enjoy a welcome breather at a splendid time of year, along with, frequently, an automatic extension for filing our taxes.

Some of these suggestions would entail the occasional dislocation. The fact that our calendar, owing to sanity saving time, would be out of synch with that of the rest of the world between February and October is one cause for concern. Strong U.S. leadership, however, could persuade many countries to adopt our system. One motto that appears on every dollar bill is *Novus ordo seclorum* — "A new order of the ages." It's time we lived up to it.

Natural Selections

—◆◆—

A N T H O L O G I Z I N G

T H E   W O R L D

EVERY FEW MONTHS, it has begun to seem, there is brought forth upon this continent, and in Europe, Asia, Africa, and Australia, yet another thick, dense volume in that long-running series of anthologies whose titles begin with the words *The Oxford Book of.* I still look forward to the arrival of these books, but I can't keep up with them anymore. No sooner have I found the time to delve into, say, *The Oxford Book of Children's Verse in America* than there appears *The Oxford Book of Prayer,* to name another recent example, or perhaps *The Oxford Book of Marriage,* or maybe *The Oxford Book of Royal Anecdotes.* There are now more than a hundred of these anthologies of prose texts and poetry. At least a dozen new ones are in the works, focused on such things as science fiction, American short stories, gothic tales, garden verse, childhood, aging, London, city life, money, villains, and the sea. Not long ago, while I was still occupied with *The Oxford Book of Royal Anecdotes* (and learning, for example, that one of Henry VIII's finger bones was made into the handle of a knife, and that one of Charles I's vertebrae was made into a saltcellar), the mail brought not one but two new specimens, *The Oxford Book of Friendship* and *The Oxford Book of Essays.* Each new tome eventually winds up on a shelf with the previous ones, temporal milestones on a long road whose end, the people at Oxford University Press assure me, I will not live to see.

I must admit that Oxford does a pretty good job with its compendia. At worst they are useful, dutiful reference books; at best they are that and also fun. To be sure, one does get the impression from time to time that an editor has managed to slip the leash and satisfy some unfortunate obsession (this might account for volumes like *The Oxford Book of Tudor Anthems* and *The Oxford Book of Australian Love Poetry*), but the subject matter for the most part has been broad, solid, and more or less of a piece with the tradition established by the first volume in the series, *The Oxford Book of English Verse*, which appeared in 1900. This tradition demands that whatever the subject matter happens to be, the material selected be wide-ranging, representative, and choice. There are now Oxford Books of French, German, Irish, Scottish, Scandinavian, Italian, American, New Zealand, and various other kinds of verse (including light, mystical, and late medieval). There are Oxford Books of short stories, of aphorisms, of dreams, of ballads. There has been an *Oxford Book of Canadian Military Anecdotes* and an *Oxford Book of English Talk*. It is hard, indeed, to imagine a subject on which people have written that has not been the focus of an Oxford anthology or that might conceivably be out of bounds.

It is this quality of relentless ambition, more than the books themselves, that I have found myself increasingly drawn to. *The Oxford Book of English Verse* was published just a few months before the death of Queen Victoria (she went down, according to an eyewitness quoted in the royal anecdotes volume, "like a great, three-decker ship"), and there is something grand and Victorian about Oxford's anthologizing enterprise, something reminiscent of one of those nineteenth-century British expeditions into the unknown to gather specimens for science and colonies for the Crown. Oxford can no longer send out her sons and daughters to colonize the world, but the anthologizing of it remains well within her power.

The impulse to anthologize must reflect something fundamental in human nature — the need, perhaps, to impose order and value, or at least the illusion of them, on a few parcels of the vast, trackless expanse of the written word; the desire, too, to set those parcels aside for the ages. How deep the impulse runs is suggested by the fact that anthologies, in the form of what today is known as a *Sammeltafel,* or collection tablet, appeared as early as the second millennium B.C., when people were still writing in cuneiform. The word *anthology* comes from ancient Greece, where its original meaning, "a garland of flowers," came to be associated with collections of poems and epigrams. Anthologies have flowered everywhere and at every period of time, and their convenience and seeming authority have made them a durable kind of work.

At their most characteristic, anthologies comfortably display a number of contradictory qualities, just as people do. An anthology is stern, reflecting a recognition that relatively little of human creation is worth saving. At the same time it is optimistic, reflecting a hope that some things *are* worth saving. And it is pragmatic, acknowledging that however many things are worth saving, there is room for only so much. An anthology may seem confident, even authoritarian. And yet it may also bow to popular will, the editor understanding that some things simply must be included, no matter what he or she may happen to think. An anthology is informed, finally, by the struggle between a wish for diversity and balance on the one hand and the nagging tug of personal preference on the other. Taken together, these strike me as a congenial jumble of stances. Most of us are capable of running through all of them in the course of a mundane task such as cleaning house or negotiating a salad bar.

In nineteenth-century England, the most popular and influential anthology of poems was for many years Sir Francis Pal-

grave's *Golden Treasury of English Songs and Lyrics* (1861). It
was this book, deemed passé by critics but still much beloved,
that Oxford University Press had in its sights when it laid plans
for *The Oxford Book of English Verse.* Oxford had two formidable assets. One was its development of India paper, which was
exceedingly thin but nonetheless opaque and which made possible the creation of a book that had many more pages than
Palgrave's anthology but remained manageable in size. The other
was Arthur Quiller-Couch, in his day known to all simply as Q
— the somewhat eccentric novelist and dandy whom Oxford
chose to be the anthologist.

Q has been described by the official historian of Oxford University Press, Peter Sutcliffe, as "not strictly speaking academi-
cally respectable at that or indeed any other time," but he had
great good sense and an enormous capacity for work. Starting
with material from the thirteenth century, he eased through English poetry like a ravenous whale, taking in great mouthfuls and
straining it through the baleen of preference and expertise, re-
taining only what he found to be meet and good or somehow
mandatory. (Q felt compelled, Sutcliffe notes, to keep Robert
Burns's "A man's a man for a' that," which he disliked, on his
initial list, because, he explained, "no Scotsman will do without
it.") The book that Q produced was a big success, and sold some
five hundred thousand copies before its first revision, in 1939.
By then Q had become in effect a professional anthologist *(The
Oxford Book of Ballads, The Oxford Book of Victorian Verse,
The Oxford Book of English Prose),* and Oxford, having seen
the money to be made, was permanently in the anthology business.

Today, of course, the editors pursue their prey with catholic
abandon. Look — over there! British political anecdotes! And
look, New Zealand plants! Welsh poetry in English! Canadian
ghost stories! Australasian verse! Death!

In the end, the most important thing about anthologies is that
they tend to survive. The roster of works of history, literature,
and philosophy that are available today because someone an-

thologized them five hundred or a thousand or several thousand years ago is distinguished. It includes much of the extant writing from ancient Israel (fashioned into an anthology called the Bible), a great deal of the ancient Greek science and philosophy that has come down to us (anthologized by the Arabs from Greek texts that no longer survive), and much of the known Middle English poetry (preserved in several medieval anthologies). It is tempting to believe that communications technology today being what it is, the danger that anything will ever again be truly lost, even when this would be desirable, has greatly diminished. Still, when I look at a shelf of Oxford Books, I can't help thinking of it as a kind of prudent safeguard — a Noah's ark (speaking of anthologies) of our civilization.

I must confess, though, to some slight worry that a few species may be forgotten. Diet books and self-help books are mainstays of modern society. Are plans afoot to anthologize them? What about personal advertisements? Or the financial disclosure statements of public servants? Or the official postmortems on technological disasters? Or the college admissions essays of notable people? Or radio talk-show colloquies? Or documents obtained under the Freedom of Information Act? Or court-ordered wiretap transcripts? I offer these in a spirit of friendly assistance, mindful that the editors of *The Oxford Book of Italian Madrigals* don't leave many stones unturned.

A License to Print Money

—◆◇◆—

ANYONE WHO has been associated with the planning of a wedding has at some point been struck by the contrasting worldviews of the couple at its core and the professionals on its periphery. For the couple, the wedding is a putatively once-in-a-lifetime event, the happy if unpredictable culmination of parallel chains of causality over the millennia. For the florists, the photographers, the caterers, the clerics, the couturiers, the bakers, and the musicians, the wedding is just a day on the job — no different, really, from thousands of other days. One encounters divergences of this kind on many important occasions (in the delivery room, at the funeral home), and it is at once disconcerting and reassuring to realize that situations of unique personal moment are to a large degree also matters of routine — that surrounding every existential exclamation point is a group of competent professionals to whom the occasion is merely a comma.

This is a lesson that the leaders of Slovenia, Croatia, Estonia, Latvia, Lithuania, Kazakhstan, and all the world's other new countries have been learning, possibly to their relief. However bloody or traumatic a country's path to independence, once independence has been achieved, the world community matter-of-factly takes things in hand.

In New York the United Nations conducts orientation programs for the new country's delegation. The mayor's office assists with the arrangements for a headquarters and housing and provides maps and restaurant guides. In Montreal the International Civil Aviation Organization approves a three-letter call sign for use by the new country's airline. In Washington the State Department elevates to embassy what was once a consulate, and makes sure that the U.S. Army Band has on file an arrangement of the new country's national anthem. The International Monetary Fund and the World Bank send missions to the new country to offer economic advice and teach its leaders how to borrow large sums of money. At the National Geographic Society, cartographers make the appropriate changes on the large globe in Explorers Hall. Here and there, émigré groups issue announcements extolling the contributions of the new country's sons and daughters. Lawyers make themselves available to write the new country's constitution, soldiers to train its military, consultants to coach its office-seekers.

One of the most important services of which new countries may avail themselves — and almost always do — is the printing of money. A society may have gotten along for years with some homegrown currency regime, such as the use of large millstones for money by the Yap Islanders, but with the conferring of independence, new countries invariably want something that can more easily be slipped to a customs inspector or a maitre d'. I hadn't realized it until recently, but no more than a few dozen countries actually print their own currencies. The rest — about a hundred and thirty countries — have to find someone to do the printing for them. As with other trappings of sovereignty, this turns out to be no problem: a handful of companies exist to do just that. The biggest, Thomas De La Rue, of London, prints currencies for about a hundred countries, including most of the members of the British Commonwealth. The United States Banknote Corporation, of New York, and Giesecke and Devrient, of Munich, each print the currencies of about ten countries. The remaining business falls to manufacturers in Canada, France, the Netherlands, Argentina, and a few other places. It's a small, close-knit world. Several dozen artisans do all the engraving, a few mills supply all the paper, one company in Switzerland supplies most of the ink, and the printing is usually done on intaglio presses built by another Swiss company, Giori.

Business is plentiful for the currency printing companies even when the world is relatively stable; because of normal wear and tear, each of the fifty billion or so banknotes in circulation at any one time must be replaced after about a year (sooner in tropical climes), at a cost of about two cents apiece. But as one might imagine, periods of chaos can be a boon to the industry. A bout of hyperinflation or counterfeiting in a country can mean that all its currency must be replaced. Political upheaval can have the same result. After the Islamic revolution in 1979, Iran decided that it wanted to replace all its paper money, because the money bore a portrait of the exiled shah. After the collapse of communism in Eastern Europe, the former eastern bloc countries replaced money that displayed Communist symbols. This sort of turnover occurs fairly regularly.

The recent outbreak of nationhood is a more unusual development, nothing like it having been seen since the era of decolonization, in the 1950s and 1960s. Croatia, whose sovereignty has been recognized by the European Community, introduced its own currency, the dinar, in 1991; Estonia, Latvia, and Lithuania followed suit with, respectively, the kroon, the lats, and the litas. The currency of all four countries was printed abroad. Although the countries whose athletes made up the Unified Team at the 1992 Winter Olympics had all stuck for the moment with the Russian ruble, they all eventually placed orders for new money. The procedures are surprisingly simple. The new country provides its printer with a list of the denominations it needs and pictures of the strange animals and arcane luminaries that are to grace the bills. It pays the company up front with some kind of real money. A few months later the country is in business, its cities awash in banknotes.

The proliferation of support services for neonations makes one wonder: has the world, without giving any real thought to the matter, made it too easy for places to become countries? An argument has roiled social science for years about whether the U.S. welfare system encourages a variety of unwholesome behaviors, and it may be time to raise a similar question about the family of nations. Regardless of the answer, it does seem that ambitious people with a few million followers who look like them and talk like them are having progressively less difficulty getting diplomatic plates for the car.

I have no wish to undo what is done; places that have gone the route of grim self-determination should be allowed to live with the consequences. But it may be useful to adopt certain criteria that prospective new countries must hereinafter meet before being upgraded, in the eyes of the world, from provisional status to true sovereignty. Several come to mind. The country must have won an Olympic medal in an event that is not the bobsled or the luge. It must be home to a filmmaker whose lyrical evocation of childhood and loss was a sleeper at Cannes. It must have a locally famous rock star who sings in the native tongue. It must at some point in its history have produced an epic poem that can now be bought in a Penguin edition. It must have the national character to have produced a cadre of vocal dissidents, and the wisdom to have eventually packed them off to Berkeley. Its army must have served with distinction as a UN peacekeeping force — outside the country itself. Two of the army's commanders must be graduates of West Point or Sandhurst. A restaurant featuring the country's cuisine must exist somewhere in the United States outside New York City.

The likelihood that a geographic entity capable of meeting these few criteria will go on to become a burden seems highly remote. Upon receipt of a hard-currency bond to ensure payment of its diplomats' parking tickets abroad, we may safely say to such a place, Welcome to the club.

The Baby Boodle

—◆◇◆—

ACQUIRING TOMORROW

TODAY

ONE DAY recently my seven brothers and sisters and I received a computerized form letter from our mother — the first time we had ever been sent such a thing. It consisted largely of a painstaking inventory of the objects in the house we all grew up in, and ended with a request: "We ask that you check those items that might interest you. Return when you can." By way of illustration, here are some of the items listed under the heading "Back Living Room":

Brass table and stand (given to Great-grandfather Murphy by the Palmers of Stonington)
Windsor armchair (Grandma Woods's only piece brought from Ireland)
Globe
Dad's bound books of illustrations
Mom's portrait
George III corner cabinet
Hammered silver service (wedding present to Nanny and Poppy)
Vase, top of corner cabinet (only piece that belonged to Great-grandma Byrne)

It was, as you might imagine, a disturbing sort of thing to get in the mail, and after tying up the phone lines to confirm that our parents had experienced no sudden change in their levels of health and sanity — normally quite high — and had simply succumbed to a fit of long-range (I hope) planning, we all turned back to the letter, and found that we had no taste for the task. I was tempted to put my initials next to the words "Mom's portrait" and send the inventory back otherwise unmarked, knowing that it would prompt a skeptical snort (and probably make for an eight-way tie), but my parents were surprisingly insistent. You don't know what it's like, they said, to have to break up a home.

On a personal level, the contemplation of such a prospect, and of the events that occasion it, is painful to almost everyone, and not easily or readily talked about. In stark contrast, to judge from recent accounts in newspapers, newsmagazines, and business publications, is the cavalier way in which the very same prospect is viewed when it can be cast as a broad national phenomenon. A younger generation — mine, as it happens — will during the next quarter-century or so supplant an older one, with consequences that have elicited slavering speculation and unseemly relish. The object of interest, specifically, is the roughly $8 trillion that the parents of the baby-boom generation are expected to bequeath to their children. This baby boodle, as one might call it, already amounts to hundreds of billions of inherited dollars annually, and the sum will grow in size every year until well into the next century.

The total amount is so large — enough to buy every share of stock of every company whose issues are traded on the London, Tokyo, and New York stock exchanges; enough to pay off the Third World's entire debt and give the 3.5 billion people who live outside the industrialized countries almost $2,000 apiece — that economists have already begun to assess the impact it will have on the national economy. Psychologists and financial planners are offering advice on how to talk to parents about their wills ("Before you broach the subject . . . know what your goals are"; "Rehearse ahead of time"). Fundraisers and philanthropies are redoubling their efforts to reach those people whose estates will ripen and fall during the coming "decade of transition" ("What to Do Before Your Donors Are Dead" was the title of a recent article in the journal *Fund Raising Management*). Advertisers have defined and targeted a demographic group that *Adweek* calls "the new inheritors." There are great expectations all around.

The hopeful tone of much of the recent writing recalls that of a speech made by Herbert Hoover in 1935, in which he assured graduating seniors at Drake University that despite the Depression all around them, they could look forward to a bright economic future. "Did it ever occur to you," he said, with what I imagine must have been a sweep of his arm toward nearby dwellings and places of business, "that all the people who now live in these houses, who conduct this vast complex of life and civilization, are going to die?"

It turns out, of course, that many presumptive beneficiaries are . . . well, impatient. They do not want to bide their time. They yearn, in fact, to exchange the frustrating and impecunious role of Pip for the more immediately gratifying one of Regan or Goneril. Some worry openly that their parents' medical and nursing home costs will drain the camel's hump, as it were. Others worry that interests and relationships forged in retirement will prompt diverting codicils (bequests to people other than next of kin are on the rise). Still others fear that the older generation will simply live on and on and on. A middle-aged man who is expecting a sizable inheritance was quoted recently in a business magazine as saying, "I feel like Prince Edward waiting for Queen Victoria to die."

What people like him need — and what someone at the University of Chicago will surely soon devise — is a futures market for inheritances. As farmers do with soybeans and pork bellies, people who anticipate an inheritance would (secretly) sign over to speculators all rights to it, in return for an immediate flat payment. For the speculator, the investment would be a risky one — the collection date, the identities of the beneficiaries as of that date, and the size of the estate when settled would all be unknowable — and the cash paid out to the person selling his or her birthright would thus probably amount to a small fraction, perhaps 30 percent, of that person's estimated prospects. But there would be many takers, I suspect, on both sides of the bargain. Before long the market in legacy futures — "full bellies," as they'd no doubt be called — would achieve a strange life of its own, subject to all the volatility that afflicts other commodities markets. Flu epidemics during a recession, which could have the effect of spurring the number of bequests at a time when estate values were soft, would send full-belly prices tumbling. Increases in Social Security and Medicaid benefits, which could prevent many older people from having to dip into savings or investments, would make full-belly prices soar. There would, admittedly, be occasional abuses — by, say, overzealous pension fund managers, who might arrange for the selective slaughter of wealthy legators at the height of a bull market — but perhaps no more frequently than they already occur in the wheat or Eurodollar market. Prudent regulation could deal with other problems. For instance, because the condition of the full-belly market would have implications for the nation's money supply and hence for the health of the economy as a whole, it would probably make sense to have a representative of the Federal Reserve Board on call at intensive care units to participate (together, of course, with the doctor and the medical ethicist) in the making of certain decisions.

The system outlined here will be criticized by some, but it undeniably would satisfy what appears to be an unmet national need. It would also put to rest all this talk about the 1990s as the "we decade." And whereas many of those who sold their birthright might well feel cheated when the actual bequest was made, one could only say, They had it coming to them.

The Last Resort

—◈◈—

WHEN ERICH HONECKER, seventy-nine, the former East German Communist leader, was spirited out of Germany in March 1992 and smuggled into the Soviet Union, he may have believed that his troubles were over. In Germany he faced manslaughter charges for a standing shoot-to-kill order he issued many years ago, under which East German border guards were authorized to kill East Germans who sought to flee to the West. Seeing Honecker's predicament, the Soviet Union, which had long been a friend to East Germany, did the fraternal thing. It took Honecker in.

And then, abruptly, the Soviet Union ceased to exist. Honecker suddenly found himself under the jurisdiction of Boris Yeltsin, the president of the newly independent Russian Federation, who responded favorably to a request by Germany, Russia's banker, for Honecker's extradition. Honecker fled to the Chilean embassy — the ambassador was an old friend — and from this sanctuary began casting about for a country where he could settle permanently. He and his wife, Margot, eventually came to realize that the countries willing to give them permanent asylum were only two: North Korea, where Erich could at least get decent medical care (he had cancer), and Cuba.

This is but the most recent episode in a long-running series in which discarded rulers of oppressive states have sought to grope their way to a globally sanctioned limbo. It is a sorry spectacle whenever it occurs, and deeply bothersome for somewhat contradictory reasons. First, on the level of principle, the fact that leaders on the lam manage to find safe haven at all means that they have eluded the clutches of justice. Second, as pragmatic observers have frequently pointed out, the fact that finding safe haven can prove difficult or impossible sometimes keeps autocrats clinging to their jobs longer than they otherwise might. Beyond those considerations is the fact that these people and their families seldom just go away. The Marcoses, the Duvaliers, the Amins, the Somozas — they make news for the rest of their lives, often while living in galling comfort and continuing to involve themselves unhelpfully in events back home.

This state of affairs is untidy, unsatisfying, and inefficient, and each frenzied new departure of an odious head of government prompts editorialists to throw up their hands and wonder if there must not be some better way. A few years ago, at a time when Panama's recent ruler, Manuel Noriega, was clinging desperately to sanctuary in the local Vatican embassy, *The Economist* suggested that perhaps the solution was to put people like Noriega and Romania's Nicolae Ceausescu "all together in a remote spot" where they could pass their days comfortably under United Nations supervision. This idea owes much to Viscount Castlereagh, who in 1815 oversaw Napoleon's successful dispatch to the island of Saint Helena, in the South Atlantic, and it has always had much to recommend it. But no concrete steps in that direction have yet been taken, perhaps for lack of firm answers to some fundamental questions. Where in the modern world, precisely, should that "remote spot" be? Should we not try to strike a balance between pragmatism and justice, offering refuge with the one hand, yes, but exacting retribution with the other? And if so, by what means can this be accomplished?

230 • J U S T   C U R I O U S

Happily, the answer to the first of these questions may have just come, inadvertently, from Fidel Castro, who has reason of late to be thinking about such things. According to an article by Benito Alonso Artigas in the Cuban émigré newspaper *Diario Las Americas,* which was brought to my attention by a friend, "The criminals Fidel and Raúl Castro Ruz have tried to rent, buy, or receive a grant of the Island of Socotra, in the Indian Ocean." The intention, apparently, is to secure a place of asylum in the event that life in Havana becomes untenable. Socotra is a wind-swept island of temperate clime that lies in shark-infested waters midway between the Horn of Africa and the Arabian Peninsula. It is mountainous; has only a small airstrip, to which there are no scheduled flights; and is inaccessible to shipping during the monsoon season. It is sparsely inhabited — cattle outnumber people — and is known in the region mostly for its superior ghee, which is a kind of clarified butter. Socotra is owned by Yemen, and if Yemen is seriously interested in selling, the secretary-general of the United Nations, Boutros Boutros-Ghali, should arrange for the UN to outbid Cuba, acquire the island, and turn part of it into a permanent homeland for deposed or weary despots. It could perhaps be known as the Last Resort.

Here is the lure: tyrants could check in at the Last Resort at any time in their careers and could bring with them as much money as they wished, no questions asked. Their persons and their fortunes would be off-limits to law enforcement agencies. The accommodations at their disposal, for which they would pay a high monthly rent, would be luxurious, and the management would make available various basic services, including a modern hospital and modern communications. Neither journalists nor tourists would be permitted on the island. The United Nations would widely publicize all these features of life on Socotra and would guarantee the world community's acquiescence (however grudging) in the basic arrangement. All in all, Socotra would probably be seen by many of its potential guests as an attractive proposition — the option of first choice in the event of job-threatening hostilities at home.

So much for the enticements. It remains to be noted that certain features of life on Socotra — the fine print, as it were — would not be widely publicized. Indeed, many of these features would become apparent only as time unfolded. To begin with, having arrived on Socotra, the former heads of government would never be allowed to leave. (Accompanying staff and family members, however, would be free to leave, even encouraged to do so — but never permitted to return.) There is also the matter of the help. None of the natives currently living on Socotra can offer quite the right background for employment at the Last Resort, except maybe in the ghee shop, so labor would have to be imported. Because Socotra would be a United Nations operation, it would make sense to award various functions to selected member states. This could be done by bearing in mind the old joke about which nationalities will be doing what in heaven and in hell. The medical care system, for example, might appropriately be run by the Russians, and the telephone system by the Irish (though the Mexicans could be asked to make the wake-up calls). All the servants at the Last Resort should be French. Complaints could be handled by bureaucrats seconded from Italian government ministries. The lifeguards would be Mongolian, the sommeliers Iranian, the meter maids from Singapore. Robert J. Lurtsema would control the public address system.

It would be natural to have the English run the kitchens, but responsibility for the cooking might in fact be handled a little differently. One promising suggestion is that each newly arrived fugitive would get to have his cooks prepare all the meals at the Last Resort until the next fugitive arrived. Thus, if Mengistu Haile Mariam were to show up, the cuisine would suddenly become Ethiopian. A year later, with the arrival of, say, Jerry Rawlings, it would become Ghanaian. The advent of the occasional alleged anthropophagite, like Jean-Bédel Bokassa, would be a culinary event. If nothing else, such a regime in the kitchen would ensure rapt attention on Socotra to news of the latest coup. The English could be compensated for the loss of the menu by being given charge of the staff's trade union.

There would have to be a bank. In one of his books, *The Getaway*, the novelist Jim Thompson imagined a bank owned by a man known as El Rey, who operates a community in Mexico where criminals in hiding can safely run to ground with their assets.

> The bank makes no loans, of course. Who would it make them to? So the only available source of revenue is interest, paid by the depositor rather than to him. On balances of one hundred thousand dollars or more, the rate is six percent; but on lesser sums it rises sharply, reaching a murderous twenty-five percent on amounts of fifty thousand and under.

Thompson's novel was published in 1958, and the dollar amounts will thus seem quaint. But the overall way of doing business would be appropriate for the Bank of Socotra. All profits would accrue to the UN high commissioner for refugees.

As long as the guests at the Last Resort have money, they can spend as much of it as they please on imports, via a UN facility to be established in Hadibu, Socotra's one harbor, and operated jointly by Lebanese accountants and the Port Authority of New York and New Jersey. However, one friend suggests the following stipulation: the money may be spent only on items native to or manufactured in a guest's country of origin. The stipulation would apply to everything: furniture, electronics, clothing, art, literature, television programs. One result would be a much-needed influx of capital from Socotra into some very poor economies. Guests on Socotra would also no doubt start praying fervently for the rapid modernization of their native lands.

What would happen when one or more residents of the Last Resort ran out of money, as the procedures of the Bank of Socotra virtually guarantee? Obviously, these people would have to find work. The local economy has little to offer, save for the job of tending the island's twenty thousand distinctive humpless kine. Perhaps a pattern would evolve whereby impoverished long-time residents would become the indentured servants of still wealthy recent arrivals. Thus, for example, Idi Amin might wind up in the employ of a newly arrived Saddam Hussein — his cooks, after all, would be needing an extra sous-chef or two for a while — who in turn might one day labor in the service of a Mobutu Sese Seko or, God forbid, a Hafez al-Assad. Upon a guest's death, any funds remaining in his account would revert to the United Nations.

To be sure, several operational matters concerning the Last Resort remain to be worked out. The day-to-day social dynamics of the establishment would almost certainly be problematic, deriving as they must from its peculiar demographics. There would be feuds, a black market, occasional bloodshed. The world, perhaps, can live with all that. On the whole, the advantages of the proposed arrangement, or some variant on it, seem clear. There is no reason, moreover, why its benefits could not one day be extended to cover international terrorists and rapacious multinational executives. And tinkering will surely introduce further refinements.

Did I mention that the lingua franca of the Last Resort would be Sanskrit? That is the language from which the name Socotra derives. It means "island abode of bliss."

Deliverance

S A F E   F R O M

S A N D W I C H E S

—◆◇—

I stood staring into the pit, and
my heart lightened gloriously.

H. G. Wells,
The War of the Worlds

ONE SATURDAY MORNING in 1962, as the school year
was about to begin, my mother convened the five of her off-
spring who were of educable age and escorted us into the kitchen.
There we were confronted by seventy-four loaves of Wonder
Bread; three plastic pails filled with peanut butter, jelly, and
mayonnaise; a hamper of egg salad; a butt of tuna fish; a hod
of American cheese; and a tube of sliced bologna the size of a
moray eel.

My mother, it seems, had grown weary of packing five lunches
a night, five days a week, for nine months of the year. By fateful
coincidence we had recently acquired a Bendix freezer the size

of an overachiever's sarcophagus, whose excess capacity could hold the 925 or so sandwiches it would take to get five children through school from September to June. We set to work at about 10:00 A.M. and put down our knives at around 5:00.

The manufacturing process went smoothly enough for a while. Each of us worked under the impression that we were creating the sandwiches that we ourselves would eat, and so the results tended to be moist and plump, with the application of condiments precisely calibrated to satisfy personal taste. We painstakingly crafted sandwiches in this way for about three hours, at the meager rate of about four sandwiches a person per hour. Then, in the early afternoon, realizing that we would be at it until well into the following week, my mother intervened. She decreed in effect that the capitalist ideal of individual initiative in the pursuit of individual reward be henceforward supplanted by an emphasis on fulfilling the quotas mandated by the School-Year Plan. Our personal luncheon stacks were nationalized; all future sandwiches, it was declared, would belong to the collective. Dispirited, we grimly resumed our task.

This is not intended as a morality tale, but it may be worth mentioning that the quality of workmanship underwent an abrupt decline. Many sandwiches found their way into the freezer without mayonnaise or indeed without filler of any kind. Nutritionists date the emergence of the dry cheese sandwich, which can be made, wrapped, and stacked in less than four seconds and which requires the use of only three minor muscle groups, to that Saturday afternoon. Inevitably, the incidence of hooliganism began to climb. Some members of our work brigade, acting with high levels of peer support, deliberately spread jelly over tuna fish or combined peanut butter and egg salad and then insinuated the noisome result into the common stock of lunch. As the shadows lengthened, we began to argue, with the same success that British labor unions were achieving at the time, that our quotas were unrealistically high. Teachers' conventions and snow days had not been taken into account. It also seemed likely that among the five of us, some thirty-five to forty days would be lost to illness; indeed, we were prepared to guarantee that they would be. In the end, as suppertime approached, my mother summarily reduced our quota to the number of sandwiches already made. The number, as I recall, was by then upwards of eight hundred.

—◆◆—

In my memories of that autumn and winter, the image of white bread, in its solid, liquid, and gaseous states, figures prominently. We learned that tuna fish and egg salad effect morphological changes in bread such that upon thawing, leavened matter achieves the fluent consistency of molten tofu. Bologna and cheese, in contrast, seem to function as powerful siccatives, causing trace elements of mayonnaise to disappear. Often we would forget to bring sandwiches up from the freezer in time for them to thaw, and these would have to sit atop a radiator at school, occasionally being turned, as fine strands of silky vapor emanated from inside the waxed paper. Sometimes, impatient, we would try to eat a partially thawed sandwich, nibbling around the soft edges until at last, its circular arctic core having been reached, further human exploration proved impossible. Needless to say, the barter value of our lunches was modest. In the scholastic economy, where sandwiches function as currency, we came to school with the gastronomical equivalent of zlotys.

There seemed to be no hope of relief. The Cuban missile crisis occurred in October but was resolved. Thanksgiving passed, Christmas passed, Valentine's Day passed. The end came, unexpectedly, in March. For some time we had vainly been calling attention to a kind of odious spotting on the surface of our sandwiches. As the spotting began to spread, we began to remark a local disturbance of the olfactory sense. Before long, as playground experiments would convincingly demonstrate, blindfolded students could detect the location of one of our thawed sandwiches, standing unwrapped, from a distance of thirteen feet, within an accuracy of a few degrees. Finally, one day we followed my mother down into the basement, where, after examining the sandwiches and uttering a long sigh, she concluded simply, "Freezer burn." To this day I regard that phrase, which denotes the infelicitous freeze-drying of a foodstuff's surface, as among the most euphonious and happy in the English language.

We waited there for a while, looking at the neat piles of expiring lunch. It was like that moment at the end of *The War of the Worlds* when, after months of horror, the narrator sees the Martians, "stark and silent and laid in a row," succumbing at last to the common cold. The cold had taken our sandwiches, too. I stood staring into the freezer, and my heart lightened gloriously.

INDEX
VVVVVVVV

were performed, 112; supposed signature of in reverse, 130
Sicking, Georgie, cowgirl poet, 54
Siu, R. G. H., progenitor of a science of suffering, 12, 14–21
siu, proposed basic unit of cheerfulness, 21
Smith, Stan, progenitor of the concept "hedonic loss," 13
social sciences: the obviousness question, 22–23; reassuring banality of much of, 23, 24
Socotra (Indian Ocean isle of), as homeland for deposed despots, 230–33
Solomon, and Worksheet D, 45
Spender, Stephen, on "third-person people," 31–32
spontaneous human combustion, 198–201
Statistical Abstract of the United States, 4
statistics: as a form of augury, 105
Stone Age lifestyle, 108–11
Stonehenge, 120–24; revised theories about, 122–23; merits of as "primitive observatory" compared with those of Oval Office, 123

Stonehenge Decoded (Gerald Hawkins), 122
Stout, Rex, 50
struldbrugs, as poor advertisement for immortality, 27
Sutter, Bruce, pitcher, 49

❦ ❦ ❦ ❦ ❦ ❦ ❦ ❦

Taylor, Robert, actor, 52
Taylor, Rod, actor, 54
teeth (human): why average size of is getting smaller, x; paleolithic Rhodesian Man described as "dentist's delight," 110; erosion of among competitive swimmers, 187
Thomas, Lowell, 50
Thomas, Zebulon, and Underground Railroad, 48
time, whether it can run backward, and may already have begun to, 106
time-space compression, 31
time-stuffing, widespread practice of, 30
Tithonous, lover of Eos, 27
Titus, Arch of, as record of plundered Jerusalem temple, 130
Tocqueville, Alexis de, mandatory citation of, 202
tortilla, face of Jesus on, 103